Air Quality Monitoring Protocol and Standard Operating Procedures for the Sonoran Desert Network

Natural Resource Technical Report NPS/SODN/NRTR-2007/003

Air Quality Monitoring Protocol and Standard Operating Procedures for the Sonoran Desert Network

Natural Resource Technical Report NPS/SODN/NRTR-2007/003

Authors
Theresa Mau-Crimmins
Office of Arid Lands Studies
1955 East Sixth Street
University of Arizona
Tucson, Arizona 85721

Ellen Porter
Air Resources Division
National Park Service
12795 West Alameda Parkway
Denver, Colorado 80225

Editing and Design
Alice Wondrak Biel
Inventory & Monitoring Program
National Park Service–Intermountain Region
12795 West Alameda Parkway
Denver, Colorado 80225

Contact
Andy Hubbard
National Park Service–Sonoran Desert Network
7660 E. Broadway Blvd., Suite #303
Tucson, Arizona 85710
Phone: 1+520-546-1607x1
Fax: 1+520-546-7601
http://www.nature.nps.gov/im/units/sodn/

April 2007

U.S. Department of the Interior
National Park Service
Intermountain Regional Office
Denver, Colorado

The Natural Resource Publication series addresses natural resource topics that are of interest and applicability to a broad readership in the National Park Service and to others in the management of natural resources, including the scientific community, the public, and the NPS conservation and environmental constituencies. Manuscripts are peer-reviewed to ensure that the information is scientifically credible, technically accurate, appropriately written for the intended audience, and is designed and published in a professional manner.

The Natural Resource Technical Report series is used to disseminate the peer-reviewed results of scientific studies in the physical, biological, and social sciences for both the advancement of science and the achievement of the National Park Service's mission. The reports provide contributors with a forum for displaying comprehensive data that are often deleted from journals because of page limitations. Current examples of such reports include the results of research that addresses natural resource management issues; natural resource inventory and monitoring activities; resource assessment reports; scientific literature reviews; and peer-reviewed proceedings of technical workshops, conferences, or symposia.

Views and conclusions in this report are those of the authors and do not necessarily reflect policies of the National Park Service. Mention of trade names or commercial products does not constitute endorsement or recommendation for use by the National Park Service.

Printed copies of reports in this series may be produced in limited quantity, and are only available as long as the supply lasts. You may send a request to:

Sonoran Desert Network
7660 E. Broadway Blvd, Suite 303
Tucson, Arizona 85710

This report is also available electronically from the Sonoran Desert Network website (http://www1.nature.nps.gov/im/units/sodn/index.htm).

When original printed copies are exhausted, copies can be obtained from:

Technical Information Center (TIC)
Denver Service Center
National Park Service
P.O. Box 25287
Denver, CO 80225-0287

Please cite this publication as:

Mau-Crimmins, T., and E. Porter. 2007. Air Quality Monitoring Protocol and Standard Operating Procedures for the Sonoran Desert Network. Natural Resource Report NPS/SODN/NRTR-2007/003. National Park Service, Tucson, Arizona.

NPS D-60, April 2007

Contents

Tables

Figures

Acronyms

ACM: Aerochem Metrics 301 precipitation collector

ARS: Air Resource Specialists, Inc.

CAGR: Casa Grande Ruins National Monument

CAL: Central Analytical Laboratory, Illinois State Water Survey

CASTNet: Clean Air Status and Trends Network

CHIR: Chiricahua National Monument

CNL: Crocker Nuclear Laboratory, University of California–Davis

CORO: Coronado National Memorial

EPA: Environmental Protection Agency

FOBO: Fort Bowie National Monument

GICL: Gila Cliff Dwellings National Monument

GOES: Geostationary Orbiting Earth Satellite

GPMN: Gaseous Pollutant Monitoring Program

GPRA: Government Performance and Results Act

HNO_3: nitric acid

IMPROVE: Interagency Monitoring of Protected Visual Environments

MOCA: Montezuma Castle National Monument

MVT: Master Version Table

NAAQS: National Ambient Air Quality Standards

NADP/NTN: National Atmospheric Deposition Program, National Trends Network

NH_3: ammonia

NO_3: nitrate

NOAA: National Oceanic and Atmospheric Administration

NOx: nitrogen oxides

NPS: National Park Service

NPS–ARD: National Park Service–Air Resources Division

ORPI: Organ Pipe Cactus National Monument

QA/QC: Quality Assurance/Quality Control

SAGU: Saguaro National Park

SO_2: sulfur dioxide

SO_4: sulfate

SODN: Sonoran Desert Network

SOP: Standard Operating Procedure

TONT: Tonto National Monument

TUMA: Tumacácori National Monument

TUZI: Tuzigoot National Monument

USDA: U.S. Department of Agriculture

VIEWS: Visibility Information Exchange Web System

VK#: Version Key Number

VOC: volatile organic compound

Background and Objectives

Background

The National Park Service (NPS) is charged with maintaining parks and their resources unimpaired for the enjoyment of future generations. Park resources affected by air quality include scenery and vistas, vegetation, water, and wildlife. Both the Clean Air Act and the NPS Organic Act protect air resources in national parks. Additionally, the Sonoran Desert Inventory & Monitoring Network (SODN) has identified several aspects of air quality as high-priority vital signs for monitoring. Over the past three decades, the NPS has developed several internal and cooperative programs for monitoring various measures of air quality that the SODN is incorporating into its program (NPS–ARD 2002).

Three main components comprise the NPS air quality monitoring program: atmospheric deposition, ozone, and visibility. Below is a brief overview of monitoring that the NPS and others are currently conducting relative to these components, and a review of that monitoring in SODN parks. Table 1 lists air quality monitoring in or near the SODN; Figure 1 shows the locations of air quality monitoring stations in the SODN region. At present, comprehensive on-site air quality monitoring is conducted at Chiricahua National Monument (CHIR), Organ Pipe Cactus National Monument (ORPI), Saguaro National Park (SAGU), and Tonto National Monument (TONT). Sonoran Desert Network reporting will summarize information from these on-site monitors. Information from CHIR monitors also may be used to characterize conditions at nearby Fort Bowie National Historic Site. Other SODN parks have no nearby monitors, and will not be included in annual reporting for air quality.

This protocol documents the methods currently used for collecting air quality data in SODN parks and provides for regular review of changes in those methods. It describes how these data are retrieved, managed, and analyzed for regular reporting to SODN parks.

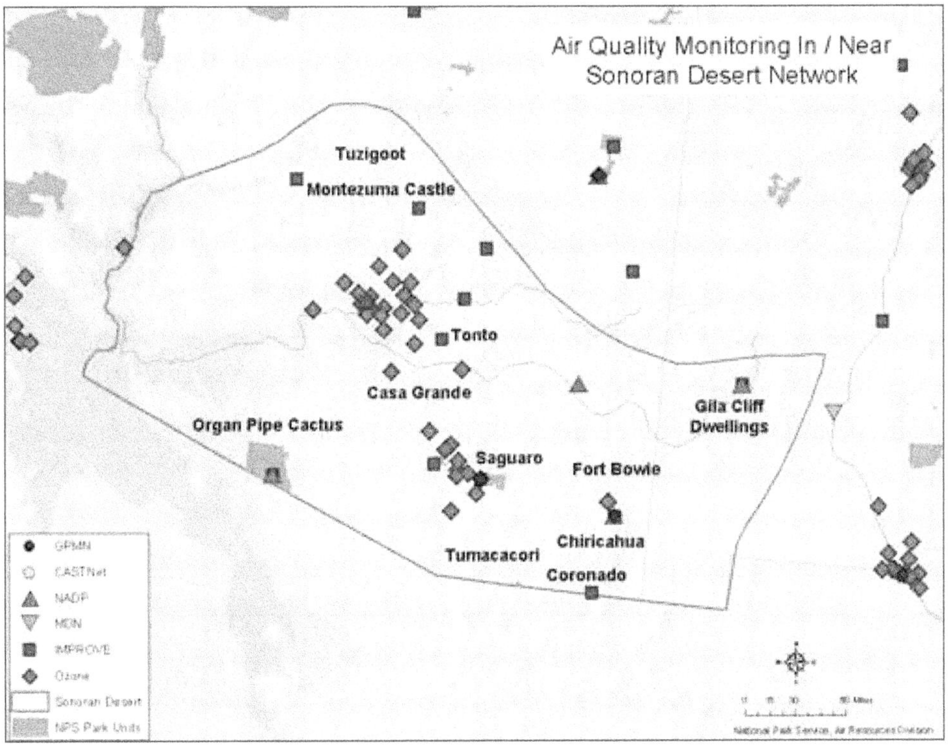

Atmospheric deposition

Wet deposition occurs when air pollutant emissions such as sulfur dioxide (SO_2), nitrogen oxides (NOx), and ammonia (NH_3) from power plants, automobiles, agriculture, and other sources are transported and transformed in the atmosphere and deposited to ecosystems as gases and particles (including sulfate [SO_4], nitrate [NO_3], and ammonium [NH_4] compounds) via rain or snow. Dry deposition of particles and gasses occurs through complex processes such as settling, impaction, and adsorption.

Atmospheric deposition can have a variety of effects on ecosystems, including acidification, fertilization or eutrophication, and accumulation of toxins. In freshwater lakes, streams, and watersheds, acid deposition from sulfur

Figure 1. Air quality monitoring stations in the SODN region.

Ozone, sulfur dioxide, dry deposition, and meteorology are collected by the Clean Air Status and Trends (CASTNet) and Gaseous Pollutant Monitoring (GPMN) networks. Ozone is also monitored with passive samplers and portable continuous analyzers. Wet Deposition is monitored through cooperation with National Atmospheric Deposition Program/National Trends Network (NADP/NTN). The Mercury Deposition Network (MDN), part of NADP, collects precipitation samples that are analyzed for mercury. Visibility is monitored as part of the Interagency Monitoring of Protected Visual Environments (IMPROVE).

Source: http://www2.nature.nps.gov/air/permits/aris/networks/sodn.cfm.

Table 1. Summary of ambient air quality monitoring in and near the SODN.

Park code	NADP/NTN Location	Site #	CASTNet Location	Site #	IMPROVE Location	Site #	Ozone Location	Site #
CAGR	ORPI 160 km SW	AZ06	CHIR 220 km SE	CHA467	Queen Valley 50 km NE	QUVA1	Chandler 50 km NW	040133009
	Oliver Knoll 180 km E	AZ99	-	-	TONT 80 km NE	TONT1	Chandler 50 km NW	040134004
	-	-	-	-	SAGU (west) 80 km SE	SAGU2	Tucson area 80 km SE	Many
	-	-	-	-	SAGU (east) 110 km SE	SAGU1	-	-
CHIR	On-site	AZ98	On-site	CHA467	On-site	CHIR1	On-site	040038001
CORO	CHIR 100 km NE	AZ98	CHIR 100 km NE	CHA467	SAGU (east) 80 km NW	SAGU1	SAGU 80 km NW	040190021
	-	-	-	-	CHIR 100 km NE	CHIR1	CHIR 100 km NE	040038001
	-	-	-	-	SAGU (west) 110 km NW	SAGU2	-	-
FOBO	CHIR 10 km S	AZ98	CHIR 10 km S	CHA467	CHIR 10 km S	CHIR1	CHIR 10 km S	040038001
GICL	On-site	NM01	CHIR 160 km SW	CHA467	On-site	GICL1	Las Cruces 160 km SE	350130019
	-	-	-	-	-	-	Las Cruces 160 km SE	350131012
MOCA	GRCA 150 km N	AZ03	GRCA 150 km N	GRC474	Ike's Backbone (Prescott NF)*	IKBA1	Hillside 100 km SW	040250005
	-	-	-	-	Sycamore Canyon (Kaibab NF)*	SYCA1	-	-
ORPI	On-site	AZ06	CHIR 310 km E	CHA467	On-site	ORPI1	Yuma 150 km NW	040270005
	-	-	-	-	-	-	Tucson area 150 km E	Many
SAGU	CHIR 100 km E	AZ98	CHIR 100 km E	CHA467	On-site	SAGU1	On-site	040190021
	-	-	-	-	On-site	SAGU2	-	-
TONT	Oliver Knoll 160 km SE	AZ99	CHIR 230 km SE	CHA467	On-site	TONT1	Phoenix area 60 km W	Many
	-	-	GRCA 260 km NW	GRC474	-	-	-	-
TUMA	CHIR 150 km NE	AZ98	CHIR 150 km NE	CHA467	SAGU (east) 70 km NE	SAGU 1	Tucson area 60 km N	Many
	ORPI 160 km NW	AZ06	-	-	SAGU (west) 60 km N	SAGU2	-	-
	-	-	-	-	CHIR 150 km NE	CHIR1	-	-
TUZI	GRCA 130 km N	AZ03	GRCA 130 km N	GRC474	Sycamore Canyon (Kaibab NF)*	SYCA1	Hillside 80 km SW	040250005
	-	-	-	-	Ike's Backbone (Prescott NF)*	IKBA1	-	-

Key to Table G1

CAGR = Casa Grande Ruins NM
FOBO = Fort Bowie NHS
ORPI = Organ Pipe Cactus NM
CHIR = Chiricahua NM
GICL = Gila Cliff Dwellings NM
SAGU = Saguaro NP

TUMA = Tumacácori NHP
CORO = Coronado NMem
MOCA = Montezuma Castle NM
TONT = Tonto NM
TUZI = Tuzigoot NM

NADP/NTN = National Atmospheric
Deposition Program
CASTNet = Clean Air Status and
Trends Network
IMPROVE = Interagency Monitoring
of Protected Visual
Environments

*Exact location unknown

and nitrogen compounds can cause changes in water chemistry that affect algae, fish, submerged vegetation, and amphibian and aquatic invertebrate communities. Deposition also can cause changes in soil that affect soil microorganisms, plants, and trees. Soils and waters in SODN parks generally have sufficient base cations to buffer deposited acids and, to date, there is no evidence to indicate that acidification has occurred or is likely to occur.

Because certain plants are better able to utilize nitrogen, nitrogen deposition can result in shifts in plant species composition. Excess nitrogen deposition can cause unwanted fertilization effects, leading to changes in plant community structure and diversity. Nitrogen additions also can result in higher plant biomass and, consequently, higher fire frequency and severity. SODN ecosystems evolved under low nitrogen conditions and are likely to respond to increases in nitrogen from deposition.

The NPS monitors the chemistry of precipitation in 42 national park units as a partner in the National Atmospheric Deposition Program (NADP) National Trends Network (NTN). Rainwater samples collected weekly using standard methods are sent to a central laboratory for analysis. Measured constituents include hydrogen (acidity as pH), sulfate, nitrate, ammonium, chloride, and base cations (including calcium, magnesium, potassium, and sodium). In the SODN, CHIR has participated in this program since 1999, Gila Cliff Dwellings National Monument (GICL) has participated since 1985, and ORPI has participated since 1980.

Dry deposition chemistry is monitored in conjunction with the Clean Air Status and Trends Network (CASTNet). Over a weeklong period, fine particles and gases suspended in the air are collected on filters that are analyzed at a central laboratory. Meteorological, vegetation, and land-use data from the sites are used to calculate deposition velocities, which are combined with the concentration measurements to estimate dry deposition in kilograms per hectare per year (kg/ha/yr) of sulfur dioxide, sulfate, nitrate, nitric acid, and ammonium.

Ozone

Ozone is a gaseous constituent of the atmosphere produced by reactions of water and oxygen with anthropogenic pollutants—particularly NOx—and by lightning. Ground-level ozone is the major constituent in smog. Ozone in certain concentrations is toxic to humans, and some plant species are particularly sensitive to ozone damage (Porter 2003). The Environmental Protection Agency (EPA) has set a national standard for ozone to protect human health and the environment. Areas not meeting the standard are designated as non-attainment areas, and states are required to develop plans to bring such areas into attainment. In the SODN region, two counties in Arizona (Maricopa and Pinal counties) are designated "non-attainment" for the ozone standard. No SODN parks are in these counties, but SAGU is adjacent to them.

Ozone is monitored using continuous samplers at SAGU and CHIR. This method employs a gas analyzer that measures ultraviolet absorbance to produce hourly ozone concentration measurements. Continuous monitoring is done as part of the NPS Gaseous Pollutant Monitoring Program, in partnership with the EPA's CASTNet program.

Particulate matter and visibility

Visibility-obscuring particulate matter consists of dust, soot, and other fine solid materials that become suspended in the air. Major sources of particulates are burning of fossil fuels, fires, wood smoke, and windblown soil. Regulatory standards for particulates and visibility include designation of non-attainment areas and visibility standards for Class I areas designated by the Clean Air Act. Two SODN parks, CHIR and SAGU, are designated Class I areas.

Visibility is monitored through the Interagency Monitoring of Protected Visual Environments (IMPROVE) Program. Fine particles of two size classes are collected on filters and sent for laboratory analysis of chemistry and mass. Samples are collected for a 24-hour period every third day. IMPROVE particulate samplers are deployed at CHIR, GICL, ORPI, SAGU, and TONT. Nephelometers (which use transmitted or reflected light to determine the concentration of particle size of suspensions) take measurements of light scattering at GICL and CHIR.

Measurable objectives

Air quality parameters are monitored in SODN park units by the NPS in cooperation with national air quality monitoring programs. Air quality data are summarized and analyzed for conditions and trends by both the NPS Air Resources Division (NPS–ARD) and the national air quality monitoring programs. Therefore, it is not the SODN's objective to replicate these analyses. Instead, the objectives are to compile the data summaries performed by these groups and provide them in a concise report to be analyzed in conjunction with other SODN vital signs. SODN air quality monitoring questions are:

- What are the conditions and spatial and temporal trends in ozone, nitrogen deposition, sulfur deposition, and visibility-reducing pollutants in SODN park units?

- How do ozone, nitrogen deposition, sulfur deposition, and visibility-reducing pollutants vary with associated vital signs (e.g., vegetation community composition, exotic plant status, climate)?

Air quality monitoring in the SODN is also conducted to allow the NPS to report to goals under the Government Performance and Results Act.

Sampling Design

Criteria for selecting air quality monitoring sites are determined by NPS–ARD objectives for system-wide sampling. Monitoring equipment is generally sited subjectively rather than following a specific sampling design. Therefore, sampling locations are not allocated so as to allow statistical inference to a broader population of sites.

Methods

Field air quality instruments are generally automated to ensure data consistency and to minimize the workload of park staff. Important exceptions are the routine replacement of sample collectors (e.g., filters, deposition buckets) and the completion of the Field Observer Reporting Form. Field operations consist of weekly visits for inspection, routine maintenance, and sample collection by park staff, and semi-annual maintenance by program specialists.

Atmospheric deposition

Wet deposition. The NPS conducts wet deposition monitoring through the National Atmospheric Deposition Program, which has more than 200 sites nation-wide funded by federal, state, and other partners. The NPS sponsors almost 50 NADP sites, including sites in three SODN parks (CHIR, GICL, and ORPI). Each site is equipped with a precipitation collector and a rain gauge. Weekly precipitation samples are collected and analyzed by the Central Analytical Laboratory (CAL), Illinois State Water Survey.

Each NADP site is required to use identical equipment: an Aerochem Metrics 301 precipitation collector (ACM) and a Belfort B5-780 rain gauge with event recorder. The electrically powered ACM automatically collects precipitation samples to be sent for analysis, while the Belfort gauge mechanically measures and records the amount of precipitation.

The NADP instrument is designed to parse wet deposition transported through precipitation from total particulate deposition (i.e., wet + dry deposition). To sort these inputs, the collector employs one "dry-side" bucket, one "wet-side" bucket, and one mobile lid that prevents one bucket or the other from receiving deposition. In the absence of precipitation, the lid seals the wet-side bucket and allows accumulation of dry particulates in the dry-side bucket. Incoming precipitation triggers a moisture sensor that in turn activates a motor that moves the lid from the wet-side to the dry-side bucket, allowing wet deposition to be collected in the former.

The dry-side bucket is not actually used to sample dry deposition, as the bucket method is not effective at sampling this fraction of the particulate spectrum. Instead, dry deposition is measured to NPS and EPA standards using the CASTNet system described below. The purpose of the dry-side bucket is to protect the rubber seal on the lid during dry periods and to serve as a fallback estimation of wet deposition and precipitation if the lid–motor system fails to operate properly.

The rain gauge serves as an independent measure of precipitation, and its event recorder records the opening and closing of the wet-side bucket in a way that can be compared with precipitation events.

The site operator has responsibility for weekly site and equipment inspection, sample collection, and completion of the Field Observer Reporting Form, where details on the sample timing, precipitation, and the status and maintenance of the equipment are recorded. Also, CAL staff may call upon the site operator to troubleshoot and repair malfunctioning equipment. Weekly sample collection procedures and routine maintenance and testing are described in the *National Trends Network Site Operation Manual* (Dossett and Bowersox 1999). Biennial site visit procedures are outlined in Dossett and Bowersox (1999). These SOPs are archived on the SODN server at V: Air Quality\Resources\References\Monitoring_Protocols\NADP, and can be accessed online at http://nadp.sws.uiuc.edu/lib/.

Dry deposition. EPA's CASTNet is the nation's primary monitoring network for estimating dry atmospheric deposition of pollutants including SO_4, NO_3, NH_4, SO_2, and nitric acid (HNO_3). For one-week intervals, a pump pulls air through filter packs that are then sent to a central analytical laboratory in Gainesville, Florida, for analysis. CASTNet uses NADP data in conjunction with dry deposition data to report total deposition. Chiricahua National Monument has the only CASTNet sampler in the SODN region; it has operated from 1989 to 1992, and 1995 to the present. The CASTNet SOPs are archived on the SODN server at V: Air Quality\Resources\References\Monitoring_Protocols\CASTNet, and can be accessed online at http://www.epa.gov/castnet/library.html.

Ozone

Ozone monitoring is conducted in two SODN parks, CHIR and SAGU, as part of the NPS Gaseous Pollutant Monitoring Program (GPMN). The GPMN uses continuous ozone analyzers configured as a reference or equivalent method specified by the EPA in Appendix D of 40 CFR Part 50. The NPS ozone monitoring protocol is available on the SODN server at C:\I+M\Air Quality\Resources\References\ARD_Protocols, and can be found online at http://www2.nature.nps.gov/air/Monitoring/docs/Final_OzoneProtocol.pdf.

Visibility

IMPROVE monitoring protocols include three types of visibility monitoring: particle (or aerosol), scene, and optical. Particle samplers, used to calculate the mass and chemical composition of fine particle matter ($PM_{2.5}$) and the mass of coarse particulate matter (PM_{10}) in the atmosphere, are located at all IMPROVE sampling sites. In the Sonoran Desert Network, CHIR, GICL, ORPI, SAGU, and TONT have fine-particle samplers. A transmissometer is currently in operation at TONT, and one operated at CHIR from 2001 to 2003. Nephelometers currently measure light scattering at CHIR and GICL.

IMPROVE particulate site operations are supervised by the sample laboratory of the Crocker Nuclear Laboratory (CNL), University of California–Davis. Particle sampling stations employ four independent sample filter modules, each with an independent pump. A single TERN 16-bit controller controls all four samplers. Operations involve weekly visits by park staff to change sample filters, verify normal operations, and inspect equipment. Park staff retrieve memory cards bi-weekly.

Sample laboratory staff also may call upon the site operator to troubleshoot and repair malfunctioning equipment. Sample filters, memory cards, and datasheets are sent to the CNL for analysis. Biennial audits are performed at each site, and equipment is calibrated annually. Field-site procedures for particulate matter sampling are described in *IMPROVE Standard Operating Procedures SOP 201 Sampler Maintenance by Site Operators* (CNL 1997a), *Version II IMPROVE Sampler Operating Procedures Manual for use in the IMPROVE Monitoring Network* (CNL 2001). These SOPs are archived on the SODN server at V:\Air Quality\Resources\References\Monitoring Protocols\Ozone, and can be accessed online at http://vista.cira.colostate.edu/improve/Publications/IMPROVE_SOPs.htm.

IMPROVE optical monitoring site operations are supervised by Air Resource Specialists, Inc. (ARS). Nephelometers in park units are Type 1 Optec NGN-2 models configured with Campbell Scientific 21X dataloggers. Park staff retrieve Campbell storage modules bi-weekly where telephone-modem data collection is not possible. ARS staff also may call upon the site operator to troubleshoot and repair malfunctioning equipment. Sample filters, memory cards, and datasheets are sent to the CNL for analysis. Biennial audits are performed at each site, and equipment is calibrated annually. Field-site procedures for optical monitoring are described in *Annual Site Visits for Optical Monitoring Instrumentation (IMPROVE Protocol)* (ARS 1996a). Procedures for annual nephelometer maintenance are described in *Nephelometer Maintenance (IMPROVE Protocol)* (ARS 1996). These SOPs are archived on the SODN server at V:\Air Quality\Resources\References\Monitoring_Protocols\IMPROVE, and can be accessed online at http://vista.cira.colostate.edu/improve/Publications/SOPs/arssop2004.asp.

Data Handling and Reporting

Data entry, verification, and editing

Data entry and data verification/validation are the responsibility of the various monitoring programs and their contractors. Each has a quality assurance plan. Their procedures are reviewed briefly below and detailed in the referenced documents.

Atmospheric deposition

Upon receipt of samples at the CAL, data from field observer report forms are entered into an R:BASE relational database. After sample processing and analysis, data from Laboratory Observer Reporting Forms are entered into the database. In each case, double-entry procedures are followed and discrepancies are resolved by the NADP database manager. Results of chemical analyses are loaded into the R:BASE database and merged with the descriptive information and metadata contained in the Field Observer Reporting Form. These procedures are reviewed in *Quality Assurance Plan*, Version 1.3, NADP CAL QA Plan 2002-01 (NADP 2002), housed on the SODN server at V:\Air Quality\Resources\References\Monitoring_Protocols\NADP and available online at http://nadp.sws.uiuc.edu/lib/#qaPlans.

Laboratory data collection for dry deposition chemistry is automated. The data management center of MACTEC Engineering & Consulting, in Gainesville, Florida, performs the laboratory analyses on the filter packs for CASTNet dry deposition chemistry. Quality Assurance/Quality Control (QA/QC) for these data (detailed in MACTEC 2003) consists, among other procedures, of verifying that values are reasonable.

Ozone

Continuous ozone measurements are recorded by dataloggers attached to the analyzers. These data are downloaded to the Air Resources Specialists, Inc., information management center daily, by modem, and e-mailed, monthly, to the MACTEC data management center, which provides them to the EPA after QA/QC procedures are completed.

Visibility

Particulate data processing and validation are performed in parallel, principally in the Crocker Nuclear Laboratory, University of California–Davis, where the samples are processed (field-site operators verify flow rates of sampler modules). The CNL data management group reviews and finalizes data, and places them on an anonymous ftp site for retrieval by end users. These procedures are detailed in *IMPROVE Standard Operating Procedures SOP 351 Data Processing and Validation* (CNL 1997b), housed on the SODN server at V:\Air Quality\Resources\References\Monitoring_Protocols\IMPROVE and available online at http://vista.cira.colostate.edu/improve/Publications/SOPs/ucdsop.asp.

Nephelometer data processing and validation procedures are described in *Collection of Optical Monitoring Data* (ARS 1993), housed on the SODN server at V:\Air Quality\Resources\References\Monitoring_Protocols\IMPROVE and available online at http://vista.cira.colostate.edu/improve/Publications/SOPs/arssop2004.asp. Details on how data are uploaded from nephelometers and maintained can be found at http://vista.cira.colostate.edu/improve/Publications/SOPs/arssop2004.asp.

Data acquisition

Data from the various air quality monitoring programs are acquired from web-based program archives. Dry deposition data are archived by the EPA CASTNet program. Wet deposition data are archived by the NADP/NTN. Ozone data are archived by the NPS Air Resources Division (only the data from in-park monitors are archived by the NPS–ARD; ozone data collected outside the parks are archived by the EPA AirData website at http://www.epa.gov/air/data/). Visibility data are archived by the IMPROVE program. Procedures for downloading these data are described in SOPs 1–4.

Metadata procedures

All national databases are accompanied by extensive metadata documents that provide details on procedures, equipment, and measurements taken. In addition to this documentation, this protocol requires that a README file be created when data are downloaded from a site. These README files, saved in the same location as the data files, document the name of the person performing the download, the date the file was created, a description of the data format and source, and any additional information that is required for a user to understand the data provenance.

All changes to this protocol narrative and SOPs are noted in a Master Version Table (MVT), which is maintained in SOP #6. Any time the narrative or an SOP version changes, a new Version Key Number (VK#) must be created and recorded in the MVT, along with the date of the change and the versions of the narrative and SOPs in effect. The VK# is essential for project information to be properly interpreted and analyzed. The protocol narrative, SOPs, and data should not be distributed independently of this table.

Data archival procedures

The SODN locally archives all data downloaded from air quality monitoring stations in their native format, designated as read-only.

Data analysis and reporting

Annual SODN air quality reports are prepared for parks with more than one type of monitoring—currently only CHIR, SAGU, and ORPI. Specific instructions for preparing annual reports are found in SOP #5. Appendix G is an example of an annual air quality report. These reports include assessments of air quality status and trends at individual sites and in comparison with the rest of the region.

Personnel Requirements and Training

Personnel are required for on-site maintenance as well as for data downloading, processing, and analysis.

Roles and responsibilities

On-site personnel, responsible for weekly visits, are staff at parks where air quality monitoring stations occur. Technical support is provided by the NPS–ARD or EPA employees and affiliated contractors. Data downloading is the responsibility of SODN data management staff; the SODN ecologist performs analyses.

Training procedures

Contractors are required to provide staff with adequate training to perform equipment inspections and calibrations. Park staff is typically trained on the job by other staff experienced with the procedures. This on-the-job training is supplemented with additional training, as needed, during site inspection and calibration visits by contractors. All laboratory analyses are performed under contract, with contractors being responsible for training their employees.

Operational Requirements

Annual workload and field schedule

Depending on the air quality monitoring equipment present, weekly visits for routine maintenance require one person for up to eight hours per week. Additional time for emergency repairs or unscheduled equipment checks (due to observed problems with data) also can require up to eight hours per week. These costs are currently incurred by the host parks, with financial support from the NPS–ARD. The costs of semiannual inspections, laboratory analyses, shipping and handling of samples, and data management are not known; these are incurred by the NPS–ARD and the EPA at a scale that is difficult to differentiate at the network level. The workload for SODN staff consists of data retrieval, archiving, analysis, and report preparation.

Facility and equipment needs

This protocol describes several ongoing programs, and is based on the assumption that the programs will continue to be externally funded. Facilities and equipment are described in the narrative above and in the SOPs. The SODN does not plan to fund additional air quality monitoring in the network park units.

Startup costs and budget constraints

There are no startup costs associated with this program at the network level. It is anticipated that this protocol will require approximately one-half of one pay period per year each for the network ecologist and data technician.

Procedures for making changes to and archiving previous versions of the protocol

Revisions to the protocol narrative and SOPs will be inevitable over time. Explicit documentation of these changes is critical for proper acquisition, processing, interpretation, and analysis of air quality data. Procedures for changing the protocol narrative and related SOPs are documented in SOP #6. The protocol narrative and all SOPs are labeled with version numbers and included in a revision history log. Changes to either document type are to be accompanied by changes in version numbers. The version numbers, dates, changes, reason for the changes, and author of the changes are to be recorded in the revision history log for each SOP. The updated version numbers must be recorded in the Air Quality Master Version Table (see SOP #6) and conveyed to the network data manager for proper updating of the master version table database. Previous versions of the protocol narrative and SOPs must be archived in the SODN Air Quality Protocol Library (V: Air Quality\Resources\ References\).

References

Air Resource Specialists, Inc. (ARS). 1993. Quality assurance/quality control documentation series: Collection of optical monitoring data (IMPROVE protocol), standard operating procedure number 4300. Ft. Collins, Colo., March.

——. 1994a. Annual site visits for optical monitoring instrumentation (IMPROVE protocol), standard operating procedure number 4115. Ft. Collins, Colo., March (rev. April 1998).

——. 1994b. Servicing and calibration of optical dataloggers (IMPROVE protocol), standard operating procedure number 4250. Ft. Collins, Colo., March (rev. May 1996).

Crocker Nuclear Laboratory (CNL). 1997a. IMPROVE standard operating procedures: SOP 201, sampler maintenance by site operators. Davis, Calif.

——. 1997b. SOP 351, data processing and validation. Davis, Calif.

——. 2001. Version II IMPROVE sampler operating procedures manual for use in the IMPROVE monitoring network v2.01.01: January. Davis, Calif.

Dossett, S. R., and V. C. Bowersox. 1999. National Trends Network site operation manual. National Atmospheric Deposition Program Office at the Illinois State Water Survey. NADP Manual 1999-01. Champaign, Ill.

MACTEC Engineering & Consulting, Inc. 2003. Clean Air Status and Trends Network (CASTNet) quality assurance project plan (QAPP), Revision 2.0. Gainesville, Fla.: MACTEC Engineering and Consulting, Inc. October, 317 pp.

National Atmospheric Deposition Program (NADP). 2002. Quality assurance plan, version 1.3, NADP CAL QA plan 2002-01, August. Champaign, Ill.: Central Analytical Laboratory, Illinois State Water Survey.

National Park Service–Air Resources Division (NPS–ARD). 2002. Air Quality in the National Parks, 2nd Edition. National Park Service Air Resources Division, U.S. Department of the Interior, Lakewood, CO.

Porter, E. 2003. Ozone-sensitive plant species on National Park Service and U.S. Fish and Wildlife Service lands: Results of a June 24–25, 2003, workshop. Baltimore, Md.: U.S. Department of the Interior. Natural Resource Report NPS/NRARD/NRR-2003/01.

Appendix A

SOP #1: Downloading and Processing CASTNet Dry Deposition Data

This SOP documents the procedures for downloading data from the Environmental Protection Agency (EPA) Clean Air Status and Trends (CASTNet) program. Instructions are also provided for creating metadata for the downloaded files.

The SODN acquires data for dry deposition monitoring stations located within SODN park units by downloading them from an EPA web site. Data management procedures follow guidelines and standards that are detailed in the SODN Data Management Plan.

To download EPA CASTNet dry deposition chemistry data:

1. Direct the web browser to the CASTNet web site, http://www.epa.gov/castnet/.

2. Select "Data" from the column on the left.

3. Select "Prepackaged Data Sets".

4. In the "Name" column of the table, select "drychem."

5. When the dialog box appears, select "save to disk". Save this file in V:\Protocols\ Air Quality\Data\Non_Spatial_Data\Raw_Data\CASTNet.

6. Unzip the files by double-clicking on the zip file and dragging the two files displayed in the new window to V:\Protocols\Air Quality\Data\Non_Spatial_Data\ Raw_Data\CASTNet.

7. Add the date to the beginning of the file names (e.g., *Dec2005_drychem.csv*).

8. Open the html file in a web browser and save in Text Only format, adding the date to the file name and changing the extension to .txt (e.g., *Dec2005_drychem.txt*).

9. Create a metadata file to accompany the raw data file.

   a. Open a new Word document.

   b. Type the following:

      Metadata for: [*filename*] (the file name created in step 4 above).

      Created by: [*your name*]

      Date created: [*mm/dd/yyyy*]

      Format: Describe the format of the data file.

      Purpose: Brief description of data and source.

      Additional info: The archive consists of a data file (.csv) and a metadata file (.txt) from the same source.

Save the metadata file, in Text Only format, as *readme_[filename]* in V:\Protocols\Air Quality\Data\Non_Spatial_Data\Raw_Data\CASTNet.

Revision History Log

Previous version number	Revision date	Author	Changes made	Reason for change	New version number

Appendix B

SOP #2: Downloading and Processing NPS Continuous Ozone Monitoring Data

This SOP documents the procedures for downloading data from the National Park Service (NPS) ozone monitoring program. Instructions are also provided for creating metadata for the downloaded files.

The SODN acquires data for ozone monitoring stations located within SODN park units by downloading them from an NPS web site. Data management procedures follow guidelines and standards that are detailed in the SODN Data Management Plan.

To download NPS continuous ozone data:

1. Direct the web browser to the URL for retrieving NPS continuous ozone data, http://12.45.109.6/. Select "Get data files."

2. On the next screen, select appropriate start and end dates for the previous 12 months.

    a. Output Format: "Comma Delimited Text File (CSV)".

    b. Long-term sites: "CHIR-ES", "SAGU-PC" and "SAGU-SH" (multiple sites can be selected by holding the Ctrl key and clicking on the sites).

    c. Parameters: Select all by first selecting the top parameter, then scrolling to the end of the list, depressing Shift, and selecting the final parameter.

3. Select continue.

4. On the next screen, confirm your selections and select "Generate Data File".

5. Save file in V:\Protocols\Air Quality\Data\Non_Spatial_Data\Raw_Data\Ozone. File names will consist of the data source name and the download date (e.g., *NPS_Continuous_Ozone_Dec2005.csv*).

6. Create a metadata file to accompany the raw data file:

    a. Open a new Word document.

    b. Type the following:

    Metadata for: [*filename*] (the file name created in step 6 above).

    Created by: [*your name*]

    Date created: [*mm/dd/yyyy*]

    Format: Describe the format of the data file.

    Purpose: Brief description of data and source.

    Additional info: Append metadata (see 7c).

    c. Select Back.

    d. In the web browser, select "Read Me". Select all (Ctrl-A), copy (CTRL-C), and paste (CTRL-V)into the metadata file.

    e. Save the metadata file, in Text Only format, as *readme_[filename]* in V:\Protocols\Air Quality\Data\Non_Spatial_Data\Raw_Data\Ozone.

Revision History Log

Previous version number	Revision date	Author	Changes made	Reason for change	New version number

Appendix C

SOP #3: Downloading and Processing IMPROVE Particulate, Optical, and Summary Data

This SOP documents the procedures for downloading data from the Interagency Monitoring of Protected Visual Environments (IMPROVE) Program. Instructions are also provided for creating metadata for the downloaded files.

The SODN acquires data for visibility monitoring stations located within SODN park units by downloading them from the IMPROVE web sites. Data management procedures follow guidelines and standards that are detailed in the SODN Data Management Plan.

To download IMPROVE aerosol data for Chiricahua NM, Gila Cliff Dwellings NM, Organ Pipe Cactus NM, Saguaro NP, Saguaro West, and Tonto NM:

1. Direct the web browser to the URL for retrieving IMPROVE aerosol data, http://vista.cira.colostate.edu/improve/Data/DataQuery/QueryWizardClient. aspx. Log in using the following information:

    a. E-mail address: theresa_mau-crimmins@nps.gov

    b. Password: sodn1234

2. Select tab 1, "Select Programs". Highlight all records beginning with IMPROVE.

3. Select tab 2, "Select Sites". Select Chiricahua NM, Gila Wilderness, Organ Pipe, Saguaro NM, Saguaro West, and Tonto NM.

4. Select tab 3, "Select Parameters." Under "Parameter Groups", highlight "Major IMPROVE Parameter", "Meteorological Parameter", and "Optical."

5. Select tab 4, "Select Dates". Highlight the year(s) and month(s) of interest.

6. Select tab 5, " Select Fields". Leave the check next to Program Code, Site Code, Date, Parameter Code, POC, and Data Value.

7. Select tab 6, "Filter Your Data". Fill in the radio button next to Non-Aggregated.

8. Select tab 7, "Format Output". Select "ASCII Text" for the format. Select "a file" for output medium, specifying the file name *improve_allparks_DATE*. Select "Delimited", "Standard format", and leave the remaining defaults.

9. Click "Submit". The file will be available for download. Save the file to V:\Air Quality\Data\Non_Spatial_Data\Raw_Data\IMPROVE.

To download IMPROVE nephelometer data for Chiricahua NM, Gila Cliff Dwellings NM, Organ Pipe Cactus NM, and Tonto NM:

1. Direct the web browser to the URL for retrieving IMPROVE optical data, http://vista.cira.colostate.edu/improve/Data/IMPROVE/Data_IMPOptical.aspx.

2. Scroll down the screen to the Nephelometer Data table and select a site (e.g., CHIR1).

3. Save the file in V:\Protocols\Air Quality\Data\Non_Spatial_Data\Raw_Data\IMPROVE\Nephelometer\GICL1. File names will consist of the data source name, location, and the download date (e.g., *IMPROVE_GICL1_nephelometer_Jan2006. csv*).

4. Create a metadata file to accompany the raw data file:

a. Open a new Word document.

b. Type the following:

Metadata for [*filename*] (the file name created in step 3 above).

Created by: [*your name*]

Date created: [*mm/dd/yyyy*]

Format: Describe the format of the data file.

Purpose: Brief description of data and source.

Additional info: The archive consists of a data file (.csv) and a metadata file (.txt) from the same source.

c. In the web browser, scroll up to the top of the page. Select IMPROVE Network Metadata. Under Programs, select "IMPROVE nephelometer (Raw). Choose site from map (e.g., CHIR1; the site circle will turn red). Under "Site Information", click on link for site code to access site metadata.

d. Select "IMPROVE Network Nephelometer"; select monitoring site.

e. Highlight all information, copy, and paste in to the metadata file with the appropriate section heading. Also copy and paste any warnings or notes posted on this web page.

f. Repeat steps 2–4e for other parks.

g. Also in the web browser at http://vista.cira.colostate.edu/improve/Data/IMPROVE/Data_IMPOptical.aspx, save the .pdf file "Nephelometer Data Description" in V:\Protocols\Air Quality\Data\Non_Spatial_Data\Raw_Data\IMPROVE\Nephelometer. File names will consist of the original file name and the download date (e.g., *Transkey_Apr2001_Jan2006.pdf*).

To download IMPROVE summary data:

1. Direct the web browser to the URL for retrieving IMPROVE summary data, http://vista.cira.colostate.edu/views/Web/IMPROVE/SummaryData.aspx.

2. Under "Summary through]most recent year] using the New IMPROVE Algorithm", select "Means for Best, Middle, and Worst 20% Visibility Days".

3. Save this file in V:\Protocols\Air Quality\Data\Non_Spatial_Data\Raw_Data\IMPROVE\Data_Summary. File names will consist of the original file name and the download date (e.g., *group_means_24Jan05_Jan2006.csv*).

4. Create a metadata file to accompany the raw data file:

a. Open a new Word document.

b. Type the following:

Metadata for [*filename*] (the file name created in step 3 above).

Created by: [*your name*]

Date created: [*mm/dd/yyyy*]

Format: Describe the format of the data file.

Purpose: Brief description of data and source.

Additional info: The archive consists of a data file (.csv) and a metadata file

(.txt) from the same source.

5. In the web browser, select "Header Description". The file should open in Excel. Select the worksheet "Group_Means", select all (Ctrl-A), copy (Ctrl-C), and paste (Ctrl-V) into the metadata file below a heading, "Header Description".

6. Save the metadata file, in text format, as *readme_IMPROVE_group_means_ mmYYYY.txt* in V:\Protocols\Air Quality\Data\Non_Spatial_Data\Raw_Data\IM-PROVE\Data_Summary.

7. In the web browser, select "Daily Values Including Patched Values" and repeat steps 1–4.

8. Select the "Daily Budgets" worksheet, select all, copy, and paste into the Daily Values metadata file below a heading, "Header Description".

9. Save the metadata file, in text format, as *readme_IMPROVE_data_budgets_ mmYYYY.txt* in V:\Protocols\Air Quality\Data\Non_Spatial_Data\Raw_Data\IM-PROVE\Data_Summary.

Revision History Log

Previous version number	Revision date	Author	Changes made	Reason for change	New version number

Appendix D

SOP #4: Downloading and Processing NADP Wet Deposition Data

This SOP documents the procedures for downloading data from the National Atmospheric Deposition Program (NADP), National Trends Network (NTN). Instructions are also provided for creating metadata for the downloaded files.

The SODN acquires data for NTN stations located within SODN park units by downloading them from the NADP web site. Data management procedures follow guidelines and standards that are detailed in the SODN Data Management Plan.

To download NADP wet deposition data:

1. Direct the web browser to the URL for retrieving wet deposition data, http://nadp.sws.uiuc.edu/nadpdata.

2. Select the link "Create a customized list for multiple-site data retrievals".

3. Input the information required by the data access authorization page.

4. On the next screen, select "Edit site list: Go".

5. On the next screen, select

   AZ06 (Organ Pipe Cactus NM,

   AZ98 (Chiricahua NM), and

   NM01 (Gila Cliff Dwellings NM), then select "Retrieve Data: Go".

6. On the next screen, select weekly data.

7. On the next screen, select the date range for the previous twelve months.

8. Select comma-delimited from the drop-down list of report formats.

9. Select "Atmospheric Deposition" under "Research/Assessment" and type "NPS monitoring" in the "brief description" window.

10. Select "Get Data." The next screen will show the retrieved data.

11. Select all (Ctrl-A), and copy (Ctrl-C). Open a new Word file and paste (Ctrl-V). The data should appear in the file.

12. Save this file in Text Only format in V:\Protocols\Air Quality\Data\Non_Spatial_Data\Raw_Data\NADP. The file name should consist of the data source name and the download date (e.g., *NADP_Dec2005.txt*).

13. Create a metadata file to accompany the raw data file:

    a. Open a new Word document.

    b. Type the following:

       Metadata for: [*filename*] (the file name created in step 12 above).

       Created by: [*your name*]

       Date created: [*mm/dd/yyyy*]

       Format: Describe the format of the data file.

       Purpose: Brief description of data and source.

       Additional info: Append metadata (see 9c).

c. In the web browser (still displaying the downloaded data), select Back. In turn, select each of the appropriate links under data documentation (i.e., explanatory notes, advisory, and delimited format). For each, select all, copy, and paste into the metadata file with the appropriate section heading.

d. Save the metadata file (Figure D1), in Text Only format, as *readme_filename* in V:\Protocols\Air Quality\Data\Non_Spatial_Data\Raw_Data\NADP.

```
Metadata for: V:\Protocols\Air_Quality\Data\Non_Spatial_Data\Raw_Data\NADP\NADP_
Dec2005.txt
Created by: Theresa Mau-Crimmins
Date created: 12-28-05
Format: Comma-delimited text file
Purpose: First download of NADP data for stations within SODN parks (1/1/78 to
6/1/2005). Downloaded 12/2/8/2005 from http://nadp.sws.uiuc.edu/nadpdata. Associated
metadata from the same source provided below:


EXPLANATORY NOTES:


DESCRIPTION OF PARAMETERS INCLUDED IN NADP/NTN REPORT OF WEEKLY CONCENTRATION DATA


 Site ID
     Alpha-numeric site identification code, first two characters of
     which are the abbreviation of the state in which the site is
     located. (For intercomparison sites this order is reversed.)


ADVISORY:
NOTIFICATION OF IMPORTANT CHANGE IN NADP/NTN PROCEDURES ON 11 JANUARY 1994
Sample handling procedures at all NADP/NTN sites were changed substantially on 11
January 1994 in order to reduce contamination from the sample shipping container.
This notification alerts you that the data for samples before and after that date
are different and not comparable. See the table below for a tabular summary of the
differences, based on a special intercomparison study. The text below describes the
rationale for the change of procedures.



COMMA-DELIMITED:
FORMAT DESCRIPTION FOR WEEKLY CONCENTRATION DATA
Delimited Format


 I. HEADINGS


 First non-blank line: Program Name
 NATIONAL ATMOSPHERIC DEPOSITION
```

Figure D1. Example metadata file for NADP wet deposition data.

Revision History Log

Previous version number	Revision date	Author	Changes made	Reason for change	New version number

Appendix E

SOP #5: Preparing an Annual Air Quality Report

This SOP gives step-by-step instructions for producing annual air quality monitoring reports by park unit. Efficient reporting of monitoring results is critical in assisting park resource managers with management decisions. An example report in the proper format is provided as Appendix G of this document. Please use the text provided in this report as a template for preparing future reports.

Annual SODN air quality reports are prepared only for parks with more than one type of monitoring, currently including Chiricahua NM (CHIR), Saguaro NP (SAGU), and Organ Pipe Cactus NM. CHIR and SAGU are Class I air quality areas. The NPS Air Resources Division (NPS–ARD) is currently developing annual "report cards" for all NPS units, based on interpolated values where air quality is not monitored. Once these report cards are available, it is recommended that the SODN use these for park units where monitoring does not take place (E. Porter, pers. comm. 2006).

It is not necessary for individuals preparing annual SODN air quality reports to have strong backgrounds in air quality. The report can be prepared sufficiently without extensive background, but the preparer is required to interpret graphs acquired from external sources. If the preparer desires more in-depth interpretation, s/he should contact Air Resources Division personnel for more information (http://www.nature.nps.gov/contact/; Ellen_Porter@nps.gov; or John_D_Ray@nps.gov).

Report format

Follow SODN Technical Report Guidelines. Numbering of SODN Technical Reports is maintained in P:\Administrative\Project_Tracking\SODN_Tech_Rpt_Numbering.xls.

Create a folder with the park name and the year (e.g., *CHIR_2004*) in V:\Protocols\Air Quality\Reports; maintain all report files here.

Report content

Reporting for each park will include air quality parameters monitored in that park. At CHIR, wet and dry deposition, ozone, and visibility are monitored. At ORPI, wet deposition and visibility are monitored. At SAGU, ozone and visibility are monitored. Table G1 in Appendix G describes which parameters are monitored in SODN parks.

Introduction

This section should not change appreciably from one reporting interval to the next.

Methods

This section will not change appreciably from one reporting interval to the next unless monitoring methods are changed.

Results

NPS–ARD summary. The NPS–ARD reports trends in air quality parameters every year, with associated statistical significance, in compliance with the Government Performance and Results Act (GPRA) for NPS sites with long-term monitoring. For wet deposition, the parameters are annual sulfate, nitrate, and ammonium concentrations for the past 10 years. A nonparametric regression technique (the Theil test) is used to determine statistically significant trends. Probabilities of ≤5% are considered to be statistically significant. Increasing or decreasing concentration trends with probabilities of ≤15% are also considered to allow for early detection of deteriorating or improving conditions.

To download the NPS–ARD summary:

1. Direct the web browser to http://www2.nature.nps.gov/air/who/npsPerfMeasures.htm.

2. Select "detailed results" and save in V:\Protocols\Air Quality\Reports using the existing file name.

3. Select Back. Right-click on the graphic displaying air quality trends in all parks and save as a .gif file for use as Figure 1 in park-specific air quality reports.

4. If possible, open the file in Adobe Acrobat (the full version, not the Reader) and extract the page with the Air Quality Trends in National Parks, *Year–Year*" graphic (Document/Extract Pages/Extract Pages As Separate Files).

5. Ascertain information from "detailed results" report for park of interest (CHIR, ORPI, or SAGU).

Use this information to prepare first paragraph of the report's "Results" section (see Appendix G and Figure G1 for an example).

Wet deposition (NADP).

Concentration data—. Because concentration is not dependent on precipitation amount, concentration data are useful for examining spatial and temporal trends.

To download concentration graphics:

1. Direct the web browser to the NADP homepage (http://nadp.sws.uiuc.edu/). Choose "Isopleth Maps", then "Annual Isopleth Maps".

2. Select the appropriate year.

3. Select both the .gif and .pdf options for "SO_4 Concentrations" (sulfate).

4. Save the files in the report folders for CHIR, ORPI, and SAGU, adding the park code, year, and "conc" to the file name (e.g., *CHIR_2004_SO4conc.gif*).

5. Repeat steps 3–4 for both "NO_3 Concentrations" (nitrate) and "NH_4 Concentrations" (ammonium).

Deposition data—. Deposition data are useful for evaluating the amount of pollutant that is delivered to an ecosystem. Deposition is dependent on precipitation amounts (deposition = concentration × precipitation), and therefore may differ significantly from year to year.

To download deposition graphics:

1. Follow steps 1–2 above.

2. Select both the .gif and .pdf options for both "N Deposition from NO_3 and NH_4" (nitrogen deposition from nitrate and ammonium) and "SO_4 Deposition" sulfate deposition.

3. Save the files in the report folders for CHIR, ORPI, and SAGU, adding the park code and year to the file name (e.g., *CHIR_2004_SO4dep.gif*).

Note: These maps will be the same in all park reports (CHIR, ORPI, and SAGU) for the reporting year.

Use this information to prepare the "Atmospheric deposition/Regional patterns" portion of the "Results" section (see Appendix G and Figures G2 and G3 for an example).

Site summary—.

To download site summary data:

1. Direct the web browser to the NADP homepage (http://nadp.sws.uiuc.edu/), choose "Data Access", and then click on the appropriate state (Arizona or New Mexico).

2. Select the appropriate site (Organ Pipe Cactus NM [SiteID AZ06]; Chiricahua [SiteID AZ98]). Gila Cliff Dwellings NM [SiteID NM01]) also has an NADP site that SODN may choose to report on.

3. Select "Annual Data Summaries", then select the appropriate year. Save this pdf file to the report file as *ParkName_Year*_NADP_Summary.pdf (e.g., CHIR_2004_ NADP_Summary.pdf).

Site trends—. As noted above, concentrations are useful for temporal trends, as they are not significantly influenced by yearly fluctuations in rainfall.

To download site trend data:

1. Repeat steps 1–2 above.

2. Select "Trend Plots".

3. Select NO_3, "mg/L" for units, and click "Create Plot". Save as *ParkName_Year_ no3_trends.mht* (Web Archive, single file; e.g., *CHIR_2004_no3_trends.mht*).

4. If Adobe Acrobat (the full version—not the Reader) is available, right-click on the image and Convert to Adobe PDF. Save as *ParkName_Year_no3_trends.pdf.*

5. Select Back, repeat steps 3–4 for NH_4, "mg/L" for units. Save the graph as *Park- Name_Year_nh4_trends.mht[/pdf]* (e.g., *CHIR_2004_nh4_trends.mht*).

6. Select Back, repeat steps 3–4 for SO_4, "mg/L" for units. Save the graph as *Park- Name_Year_so4_trends.mht[/pdf]* (e.g., *CHIR_2004_so4_trends.mht*).

A link to "Trends notes" describes how the trend lines were created and discusses data completeness criteria.

Use this information to prepare the "Atmospheric deposition/Site trends" portion of the "Results" section (see Appendix G and Figure G4 for an example).

Dry deposition (CASTNet).

Trends and composition—. To download dry deposition trends and composition data:

1. Direct the web browser to CASTNet's homepage (http://www.epa.gov/castnet/), select "Site Information," then select Chiricahua NM from the site list or from the map.

2. Click on the graph labeled "Trends in total sulfur deposition", save as *CHIR_Year_ totalS_castnet.gif.*

3. If Adobe Acrobat (the full version—not the Reader) is available, right-click on the image and Convert to Adobe PDF. Save as *CHIR_Year_totalS_castnet.pdf.*

4. Select Back, repeat steps 2–3 for the graph labeled, "Trends in total nitrogen depo-

sition". Save this image as *CHIR_Year_totalN_castnet.gif[/pdf]*.

5. Select Back, repeat steps 2–3 for the pie chart labeled, "Composition of total sulfur deposition by species". Save this image as *ParkName_Year_sdep_castnet* (e.g., *CHIR_2004_sdep_ castnet.gif[/pdf]*).

6. Select Back, repeat steps 2–3 for the pie chart labeled, "Composition of total nitrogen deposition by species". Save this image as *ParkName_Year_ndep_castnet. gif[/pdf]* (e.g., *CHIR_2004_ndep_castnet.gif*).

Use this information to prepare the "Atmospheric deposition/Site trends" portion of the "Results" section (see Appendix G and Figures G5 and G6 for an example).

Ozone. The NPS–ARD reports ozone and meteorological data annually for the Gaseous Pollutant Monitoring Network and parks with state-operated ozone monitoring.

To download ozone data:

1. Direct the web browser to http://www2.nature.nps.gov/air/Monitoring/ads/AD-SReport.cfm.

2. Select the desired year and Submit.

3. Save the file in both the CHIR and SAGU report folders (V:\Protocols\Air Quality\Reports*ParkName_Year*\) with the file name *ARD_Annual_Data_Summary_year. pdf*.

Ground-level ozone is monitored in two SODN park units, CHIR and SAGU. In a table like the one shown in Table G2, fill in the values for how valid the sensors were at the park units, based on the NPS–ARD table, "Data Collections Statistics by Site".

In a table like the one shown in Table G2, fill in the listed values for the following table based on values found in the NPS–ARD table, "Summary of Ozone Data by Site" (# Days with 8-Hour Average O_3 Values >85 ppb, 1st Hi 8-hr, 4th Hi 8-hr); figure, "Annual Second Highest 1-Hour Average Ozone Concentrations (in ppb)" (2nd Hi 1-hr); and table, "Summary of Indices for Resource Injury" (SUM06 (ppm-hr)).

Use this information to prepare the "Ozone" portion of the "Results" section (see Appendix G and Table G2 for an example).

IMPROVE.

Spatial and seasonal trends—. To download spatial and seasonal trends data for Chiricahua NM, Gila Cliff Dwellings NM, Organ Pipe Cactus NM, Saguaro NP, and Tonto NM:

1. Direct the web browser to the VIEWS website (http://vista.cira.colostate.edu/views/). On the left, under Annual Summary, select "Spatial Patterns".

2. Select "Worst 20% days", "aerosol_bext", and year of interest.

3. Click on park of interest. The map will take a while to load.

4. Right-click on the map and save in V:\Protocols\Air Quality\Reports as *Parkname_Year_bext_Worst20Map.gif* (e.g., *CHIR_2004_bext_Worst20Map.gif*).

5. If Adobe Acrobat (the full version—not the Reader) is available, right-click on the image and Convert to Adobe PDF. Save as *Parkname_Year_ bext_Worst20graph. pdf*.

6. Repeat steps 4–5 for the bar graph below the map. Save as *Parkname_Year_ bext_Worst20graph.gif[/pdf]* (e.g., *CHIR_2004_bext_Worst20graph.gif*).

7. Select "Best 20% days". The map will update automatically but, again, takes a while. Repeat steps 4–6. Save as *Parkname_Year_ bext_Best20graph.gif[/pdf]*.

Use this information to prepare the "Visibility/Spatial and seasonal trends" portion of the "Results" section (see Appendix G, Table G3, and Figures G7 and G8 for an example).

Site trends—. To download site trends data:

1. Direct the web browser to Direct the web browser to the VIEWS website (http://vista.cira.colostate.edu/views/). On the left, under Annual Summary, select "Trends".

2. Under "Site Selection/Site Selection Panel," select "Show".

3. Select the park(s) of interest.

4. Under "Parameters," select "aerosol_bext".

5. Under "Aggregations" select "Best 20%", "Worst 20%", and "1 Year" moving average.

6. Under "Display Options" select "Timeline" chart and "Line".

7. Select "Update".

8. Right-click on the map and save in V:\Protocols\Air Quality\Reports as *Park-Name_bext_trends_Date.png* (e.g., *CHIR_2004_bext_Worst20Map.png*).

9. If Adobe Acrobat (the full version—not the Reader) is available, right-click on the image and Convert to Adobe PDF. Save as *ParkName_bext_trends_Date.pdf*.

10. Open ("Show") spreadsheet under graph; note value of aerosol_bext for 20% worst days. This value is the average light extinction value for the 20% worst days and can be used in visibility discussion to summarize annual information. Also note the value of aerosol_bext for 20% best days.

Use this information to prepare the "Visibility/Site trends" portion of the "Results" section (see Appendix G and Figure G9 for an example).

Composition of visibility-reducing fine particles—. To download particle data and graphs:

1. Direct the web browser to the VIEWS website (http://vista.cira.colostate.edu/views/). On the left, under Annual Summary, select "Composition".

2. Under "Site Selection/Site Selection Panel," select "Show".

3. Select the park(s) of interest, update chart.

4. Right-click on the bar chart and save in V:\Protocols\Air Quality\Reports as *Park-Name_hazecomp_Date.png* (e.g., *CHIR_hazecomp_2-2006.png*).

5. If Adobe Acrobat (the full version—not the Reader) is available, right-click on the image and Convert to Adobe PDF. Save as *ParkName_hazecomp_Date.pdf*.

6. Repeat steps 5–6 for the pie charts. Save as *ParkName_hazecomp_piechart_Date. png[/pdf]*.

Use this information to prepare the "Visibility/Composition" portion of the "Results" section (see Appendix G and Figures G10 and G11 for an example).

Discussion and Conclusions

Briefly describe the status and trends of each of the air quality parameters using the text in the example report (Appendix G) as a template. If you desire more in-depth discussion or interpretation of a particular parameter, contact Air Resources Division personnel for assistance (http://www.nature.nps.gov/contact/; Ellen_Porter@nps.gov, or John_D_Ray@ nps.gov).

Revision History Log

Previous version number	Revision date	Author	Changes made	Reason for change	New version number

Appendix F

SOP #6: Revising the Protocol Narrative and SOPs

This Standard Operating Procedure explains how to make and track changes to the Air Quality Monitoring Protocol Narrative and associated SOPs for the Sonoran Desert Network (SODN) units of the National Park Service (NPS). The protocol narrative and SOPs were based on existing procedures for acquiring air quality data, and on current perceptions of the types of analyses and reports most useful to park managers and researchers. However, the protocol narrative and SOPs will require modifications as sensors, equipment, laboratory procedures, data retrieval capabilities, and information needs change. Changes should be evaluated first in terms of cost and benefit, then subjected to appropriate review and, if approved, implemented in a timely manner.

SOP #6 must be followed when making changes to ensure that previous data collection and processing procedures are clearly understood when using and interpreting historical datasets. Similarly, clearly articulating new methods is key to credible interpretation of data acquired since the implementation of changes. Personnel making changes must be familiar with this SOP to ensure that proper reviews are conducted and that documentation standards are followed.

Procedures

1. **Data collection and availability.** The SODN air quality monitoring effort relies on existing stations that are sponsored by various national programs. Tracking changes in data collection methods and data availability will require data management staff to frequently review air quality station metadata and data availability. Station metadata should be reviewed at least once each year. Metadata sources are shown in Table F1. Data access evaluation is accomplished through the annual acquisition of air quality data (as outlined in SOPs #1–4) and documentation of changes in data access policies.

2. **Review.** Modifications must be reviewed for clarity and technical soundness. Small changes or additions to existing methods will be reviewed in-house by SODN Inventory & Monitoring staff. An outside review is required for substantive changes to methods. Regional and national NPS staff and outside experts familiar with air quality monitoring and data analysis will review major changes.

3. **Documentation.** All changes must be documented. Updated protocol revisions must be recorded in the Revision History Log that accompanies the protocol narrative and each SOP. Changes are recorded only in the protocol narrative or the SOP being modified. Version numbers will increase incrementally by hundredths (e.g., version 1.01, version 1.02, etc.) for minor changes. Major revisions will be designated with the next whole number (e.g., version 2.0, 3.0, 4.0, etc.). The following must be recorded: previous version number, date of revision, author of revision, paragraphs and pages where changes are made, and reason for the changes along with the new version number.

4. **Master Version Table.** Narrative and SOP updates may occur independently. That is, a change in one SOP will not necessarily invoke changes in other SOPs; a narrative update may not require SOP modifications. All narrative and SOP version changes must be noted in the Master Version Table (MVT), which is maintained in this SOP. Any time a narrative or an SOP version change occurs, a new Version Key Number (VK#) must be created and recorded in the MVT, along with the date of the change and the versions of the narrative and SOPs in effect. The VK# increases by increments of

Table F1. Metadata sources for air quality programs in the SODN park units.

Air quality station	Source
National Trends Network (NADP)	http://nadp.sws.uiuc.edu/lib
CASTNet	http://www.epa.gov/castnet/
NPS Ozone	http://www2.nature.nps.gov/air/Monitoring/ads/ADSReport.cfm
IMPROVE	http://vista.cira.colostate.edu/improve/Data/IMPROVE/improve_data.htm

whole integers (e.g., 1, 2, 3, 4, 5). Updates to the MVT must also be provided to the SODN data manager for inclusion in the master version table database. The VK# is essential for project information to be properly interpreted and analyzed. **The protocol narrative, SOPs, and data should not be distributed independently of this table.**

5. **Record-keeping.** Previous versions of the protocol narrative and SOPs must be archived in the SODN Air Quality Protocol Library.

Revision History Log

Previous version number	Revision date	Author	Changes made	Reason for change	New version number

Master Version Table

Version Key #	Date of change	Narrative	SOP #1	SOP #2	SOP #3	SOP #4	SOP #5	SOP #6

2005 Air Quality Monitoring Report:
Chiricahua National Monument

Theresa Mau-Crimmins
Sonoran Desert Inventory & Monitoring Network
[Address]

Ellen Porter
National Park Service Air Resources Division
[Address]

[Date]

Report-appropriate photo here

Introduction

The National Park Service (NPS) is charged with maintaining parks and their resources unimpaired for the enjoyment of future generations. Park resources affected by air quality include scenery and vistas, vegetation, water, and wildlife. Both the NPS Organic Act and the Clean Air Act protect air resources in national parks. Two Sonoran Desert Network Inventory & Monitoring Network (SODN) parks, Chiricahua National Monument (CHIR) and Saguaro National Park (SAGU), are classified as Class I air quality areas and receive the highest protection under the Clean Air Act. The SODN has identified several aspects of air quality as high-priority vital signs for monitoring: atmospheric deposition, ozone, and visibility. Over the past three decades, the NPS has developed several internal and cooperative programs for monitoring these measures of air quality that the SODN is incorporating into its program (NPS–ARD 2002).

All three components of the NPS air quality monitoring program (atmospheric deposition, ozone, and visibility) are monitored in Chiricahua National Monument. This report summarizes the results of that monitoring for 2004.

Monitoring objectives

The NPS monitors air quality parameters in SODN park units in cooperation with national programs. Air quality data are summarized and analyzed for conditions and trends by both the NPS Air Resources Division (NPS–ARD) and the national air quality monitoring programs. Therefore, it is not the SODN's objective to replicate these analyses. Instead, the objectives are to compile the data summaries performed by these groups and provide them in a concise report to be analyzed in conjunction with other SODN vital signs. SODN air quality monitoring questions are:

- What are the conditions and spatial and temporal trends in ozone, nitrogen deposition, sulfur deposition, and visibility-reducing pollutants in SODN park units?

- How do ozone, nitrogen deposition, sulfur deposition, and visibility-reducing pollutants vary with associated vital signs (e.g., vegetation community composition, exotic plant status, climate)?

Government Performance and Results Act Goal Ia3

Air quality monitoring in the SODN is also conducted to allow the NPS to report on goals under the Government Performance and Results Act (GPRA). Long-term GPRA Air Quality Goal Ia3 states that by September 30, 2008, air quality in 70% of reporting park areas will have remained stable or improved. Interim goals also have been established. For example, the goal for 2005 was that by September 30, air quality in 64% of reporting park areas had remained stable or improved (in fact, 68% of reporting park areas met this goal; NPS 2005). Six measures for three performance indicators (visibility, ozone, and wet deposition) are tracked. The NPS–ARD reports annually on the trend of these measures and whether individual parks meet Goal Ia3.

Background

Although this report focuses on monitoring in Chiricahua National Monument, the NPS and other federal and state agencies also conduct monitoring at additional locations in the SODN region. Table G1 lists air quality monitoring in or near the SODN. Individual monitoring programs are described below.

Atmospheric deposition

Wet deposition

Wet deposition occurs when air pollutant emissions such as sulfur dioxide (SO_2), nitrogen oxides (NOx), and ammonia (NH_3) from power plants, automobiles, agriculture, and other sources are transported and transformed in the atmosphere and deposited to ecosystems as gases and particles (including sulfate [SO_4], nitrate [NO_3], and ammonium [NH_4] compounds) via rain or snow.

Deposition of sulfur and nitrogen compounds may have adverse effects on ecosystems. Both are potentially acidifying to soils and waters (though soils and waters in SODN parks generally have sufficient base cations to buffer deposited acids and, to date, there is no evidence

---

Key to Table G1

CAGR = Casa Grande Ruins NM
FOBO = Fort Bowie NHS
ORPI = Organ Pipe Cactus NM
CHIR = Chiricahua NM
GICL = Gila Cliff Dwellings NM
SAGU = Saguaro NP

TUMA = Tumacácori NHP
CORO = Coronado NMem
MOCA = Montezuma Castle NM
TONT = Tonto NM
TUZI = Tuzigoot NM

NADP/NTN = National Atmospheric Deposition Program

CASTNet = Clean Air Status and Trends Network

IMPROVE = Interagency Monitoring of Protected Visual Environments

*Exact location unknown

Table G1. Summary of ambient air quality monitoring in and near the SODN.

Park code	NADP/NTN		CASTNet		IMPROVE		Ozone	
	Location	Site #	Location	Site #	Location	Site #	Location	Site #
CAGR	ORPI 160 km SW	AZ06	CHIR 220 km SE	CHA467	Queen Valley 50 km NE	QUVA1	Chandler 50 km NW	040133009
	Oliver Knoll 180 km E	AZ99	-	-	TONT 80 km NE	TONT1	Chandler 50 km NW	040134004
	-		-	-	SAGU (west) 80 km SE	SAGU2	Tucson area 80 km SE	Many
	-		-	-	SAGU (east) 110 km SE	SAGU1	-	-
CHIR	On-site	AZ98	On-site	CHA467	On-site	CHIR1	On-site	040038001
CORO	CHIR 100 km NE	AZ98	CHIR 100 km NE	CHA467	SAGU (east) 80 km NW	SAGU1	SAGU 80 km NW	040190021
	-	-	-	-	CHIR 100 km NE	CHIR1	CHIR 100 km NE	040038001
	-	-	-	-	SAGU (west) 110 km NW	SAGU2	-	-
FOBO	CHIR 10 km S	AZ98	CHIR 10 km S	CHA467	CHIR 10 km S	CHIR1	CHIR 10 km S	040038001
GICL	On-site	NM01	CHIR 160 km SW	CHA467	On-site	GICL1	Las Cruces 160 km SE	350130019
	-	-	-	-	-	-	Las Cruces 160 km SE	350131012
MOCA	GRCA 150 km N	AZ03	GRCA 150 km N	GRC474	Ike's Backbone (Prescott NF)*	IKBA1	Hillside 100 km SW	040250005
	-	-	-	-	Sycamore Canyon (Kaibab NF)*	SYCA1	-	-
ORPI	On-site	AZ06	CHIR 310 km E	CHA467	On-site	ORPI1	Yuma 150 km NW	040270005
	-	-	-	-	-	-	Tucson area 150 km E	Many
SAGU	CHIR 100 km E	AZ98	CHIR 100 km E	CHA467	On-site	SAGU1	On-site	040190021
	-	-	-	-	On-site	SAGU2	-	-
TONT	Oliver Knoll 160 km SE	AZ99	CHIR 230 km SE	CHA467	On-site	TONT1	Phoenix area 60 km W	Many
	-	-	GRCA 260 km NW	GRC474	-	-	-	-
TUMA	CHIR 150 km NE	AZ98	CHIR 150 km NE	CHA467	SAGU (east) 70 km NE	SAGU 1	Tucson area 60 km N	Many
	ORPI 160 km NW	AZ06	-	-	SAGU (west) 60 km N	SAGU2	-	-
	-	-	-	-	CHIR 150 km NE	CHIR1	-	-
TUZI	GRCA 130 km N	AZ03	GRCA 130 km N	GRC474	Sycamore Canyon (Kaibab NF)*	SYCA1	Hillside 80 km SW	040250005
	-	-	-	-	Ike's Backbone (Prescott NF)*	IKBA1	-	-

to indicate that acidification has occurred or is likely to occur). Nitrogen compounds can have a fertilizing effect on ecosystems, and because certain plants are better able to utilize nitrogen, nitrogen deposition can result in shifts in plant species composition. Nitrogen additions also can result in higher plant biomass and, consequently, higher fire frequency and severity, and may favor invasive alien species over native species (Fenn et al. 2003; Brooks 2003). SODN ecosystems evolved under low nitrogen conditions and are likely to respond to increases in nitrogen from deposition.

There are currently no U.S. standards for atmospheric deposition. Europe and Canada have established "critical loads" for deposition to protect and restore ecosystems, and the NPS, Environmental Protection Agency (EPA), and other agencies are currently exploring the potential for using the critical load approach in this country.

The NPS conducts wet deposition monitoring through the National Atmospheric Deposition Program (NADP), which has more than 200 sites nationwide funded by federal, state, and other partners. The NPS sponsors almost 50 NADP sites, including sites in two SODN parks (CHIR and Organ Pipe Cactus National Monument). The New Mexico Environment Department and EPA sponsor an NADP site at a third SODN park, Gila Cliff Dwellings National Monument. Each site is equipped with a precipitation collector and a rain gauge. Weekly precipitation samples are collected and analyzed by the Central Analytical Laboratory–Illinois State Water Survey. The CHIR NADP site has been operating since 1999.

Dry deposition

Dry deposition of particles and gasses occurs by complex processes such as settling, impaction, and adsorption. The EPA Clean Air Status and Trends Network (CASTNet) is the nation's primary monitoring network for estimating dry atmospheric deposition of pollutants including SO_4, NO_3, NH_4, SO_2, and nitric acid (HNO_3). For one-week intervals, a pump pulls air through filter packs that are then sent to a central analytical laboratory in Gainesville, Florida, for analysis. CASTNet uses NADP data in conjunction with dry deposition data to report total deposition. Chiricahua NM has the only CASTNet sampler in the SODN region; it has operated from 1989 to 1992, and 1995 to the present.

Ozone

Ground-level ozone, produced by the reaction of NOx and volatile organic compounds (VOCs) in the presence of sunlight, is one of the most widespread pollutants affecting vegetation and public health in the U.S. Combustion processes from power plants, automobiles, and industries are the main anthropogenic emitters of NOx. Vehicles, industries, and natural vegetation emit VOCs. Exposure to ozone affects human health, causing acute respiratory problems, aggravation of asthma, temporary decreases in lung capacity in some adults, inflammation of lung tissue, and impairment of the body's immune system. Ozone also affects vegetation, including both agricultural crop species and natural species in national parks.

Although ozone is generally viewed as an urban problem, ozone and its precursor emissions can travel long distances, resulting in elevated ozone levels in national parks. Ozone is monitored in two SODN parks, CHIR (1992–present) and SAGU (1982–present).

To protect human health and public welfare, the EPA has set an ozone national ambient air quality standard (NAAQS) of 85 parts per billion (ppb) averaged over an 8-hour period. Compliance with the standard occurs if the three-year average of the fourth-highest daily maximum 8-hour average ozone concentrations measured at a monitor over the course of one year does not exceed 0.08 parts per million (ppm), or 85 ppb (see http://www.epa.gov/air/criteria.html for full details). Areas not meeting the standard are designated as non-attainment areas, and states are required to develop plans to bring such areas into attainment. In the SODN region, two counties in Arizona (Maricopa and Pinal) are designated non-attainment for the ozone standard. No SODN parks are in these counties, but Saguaro NP is adjacent to Pinal County.

Visibility

Visibility includes not only how far we can see, but how well we can see. Visibility is often expressed in terms of light extinction measured in inverse megameters (Mm^{-1}). Small pollutant particles in the air scatter and absorb light, causing haze and reducing visibility. As light extinction increases, visibility decreases.

Visibility in Class I air quality areas has been granted special protection under the Clean Air Act. The "regional haze" regulations require states to establish goals for each Class I area to improve visibility on the haziest 20% of days and ensure that no degradation occurs on the best 20% of days. Natural visibility conditions are to be achieved in these areas by 2064. Visibility is monitored in parks and wilderness areas as part of the Interagency Monitoring of Protected Visual Environments (IMPROVE) program. IMPROVE is a cooperative effort that includes the EPA, U.S. Forest Service, NPS, U.S. Fish and Wildlife Service, Bureau of Land Management,

National Oceanic and Atmospheric Administration, and several interstate air quality management organizations.

Methods

Atmospheric deposition

Atmospheric deposition is monitored in the SODN by the NADP and CASTNet. Because of differences between wet and dry deposition, NADP's and CAST-Net's monitoring and analysis methods are different. The NADP collects rainfall and analyzes the sample for cations and anions, reporting concentrations of those constituents in milligrams per liter of rainfall. Rainfall amount is factored in to estimate deposition rates in kilogram per hectare per year. The NADP reports individual site data and produces isopleth maps of wet deposition concentrations and deposition.

CASTNet uses filters to collect atmospheric particles suspended in the air, analyzes the filters, and reports concentrations in micrograms per cubic meter of air. An inferential model is then applied to estimate deposition in kilograms per hectare per year. Because the inferential model is very site-specific (e.g., dependent on vegetation types), CASTNet does not recommend extrapolating the dry deposition data between areas, and does not produce isopleth maps of deposition as NADP does.

The NADP maps of interpolated wet deposition values are useful for examining spatial differences in the loadings of pollutants to ecosystems. NADP concentration data (as opposed to deposition data) are typically used to track temporal trends in the components of deposition. Deposition data are less useful for tracking temporal trends because deposition is affected by annual variations in rainfall amounts. CASTNet has recently started reporting both dry and wet (from NADP) deposition data, providing total deposition estimates for areas with CASTNet samplers.

Ozone

In addition to harming human health, research shows that certain plant species are more sensitive than humans to ozone, and that effects on plants occur well below the NAAQS. Scientists use various exposure indices to quantify ozone exposure to plants—indices considered biologically relevant because they take into account both peak ozone concentrations and cumulative exposure to ozone. These indices include the SUM06 (the running, 90-day maximum sum of the 0800–2000 hourly concentrations of ozone equal to or greater than 0.06 ppm) and the W126 (the weighted sum of the 24 one-hour ozone concentrations daily from April through October, with

the N100, i.e., number of hours ≥100 ppb). In general, both indices—SUM06 and W126 with N100—need to be satisfied in order to have a moderate-to-high risk for ozone injury, and soil moisture needs to be sufficient so that plant stomates are likely to be open and ozone is able to enter the leaf. More information on these indices can be found in the ozone injury risk assessment for the SODN at http://www2.nature.nps.gov/air/Pubs/pdf/03Risk/sodnO3RiskOct04.pdf (NPS–ARD 2004).

Ozone monitoring is conducted in two SODN parks, CHIR and SAGU, as part of the NPS Gaseous Pollutant Monitoring Program (GPMN). The GPMN uses continuous ozone analyzers configured as a reference or equivalent method specified by the EPA in Appendix D of 40 CFR Part 50. The NPS ozone monitoring protocol is available on the SODN server at C:\I+M\Air Quality\Resources\References\ARD_Protocols, and can be found online at http://www2.nature.nps.gov/air/Monitoring/docs/Final_OzoneProtocol.pdf.

Visibility

IMPROVE monitoring protocols include three types of visibility monitoring: particle (or aerosol), scene, and optical. Particle samplers are located at all IMPROVE sampling sites and are used to calculate the mass and chemical composition of fine particle matter ($PM_{2.5}$) and the mass of coarse particulate matter (PM_{10}) in the atmosphere. In the SODN, Chiricahua NM, Gila Cliff Dwellings NM, Organ Pipe Cactus NM, Saguaro NP, and Tonto NM have fine particle samplers. The sampler at CHIR has operated from 1988 to the present. CHIR also has optical monitoring, using a nephelometer to measure light scattering (2003–present).

Results

The NPS's FY2005 GPRA report (NPS 2005) addressed air quality trends in parks nationwide with long-term monitoring from 1995–2004. Chiricahua NM reported on ozone and visibility parameters, showing an improving trend for visibility on clear days and no trend for visibility on hazy days or ozone during that period (Figure G1). Therefore, CHIR met NPS Air Quality GPRA Goal Ia3. CHIR's data record was not long enough to report on wet deposition (to report to GPRA, a site must have at least six years in the 10-year reporting period for a given parameter). The map indicates that some parks in the Intermountain West degraded in terms of nitrogen deposition (nitrate, ammonium, or both), ozone, and visibility.

Conditions and trends in individual air quality parameters at CHIR are described in more detail below.

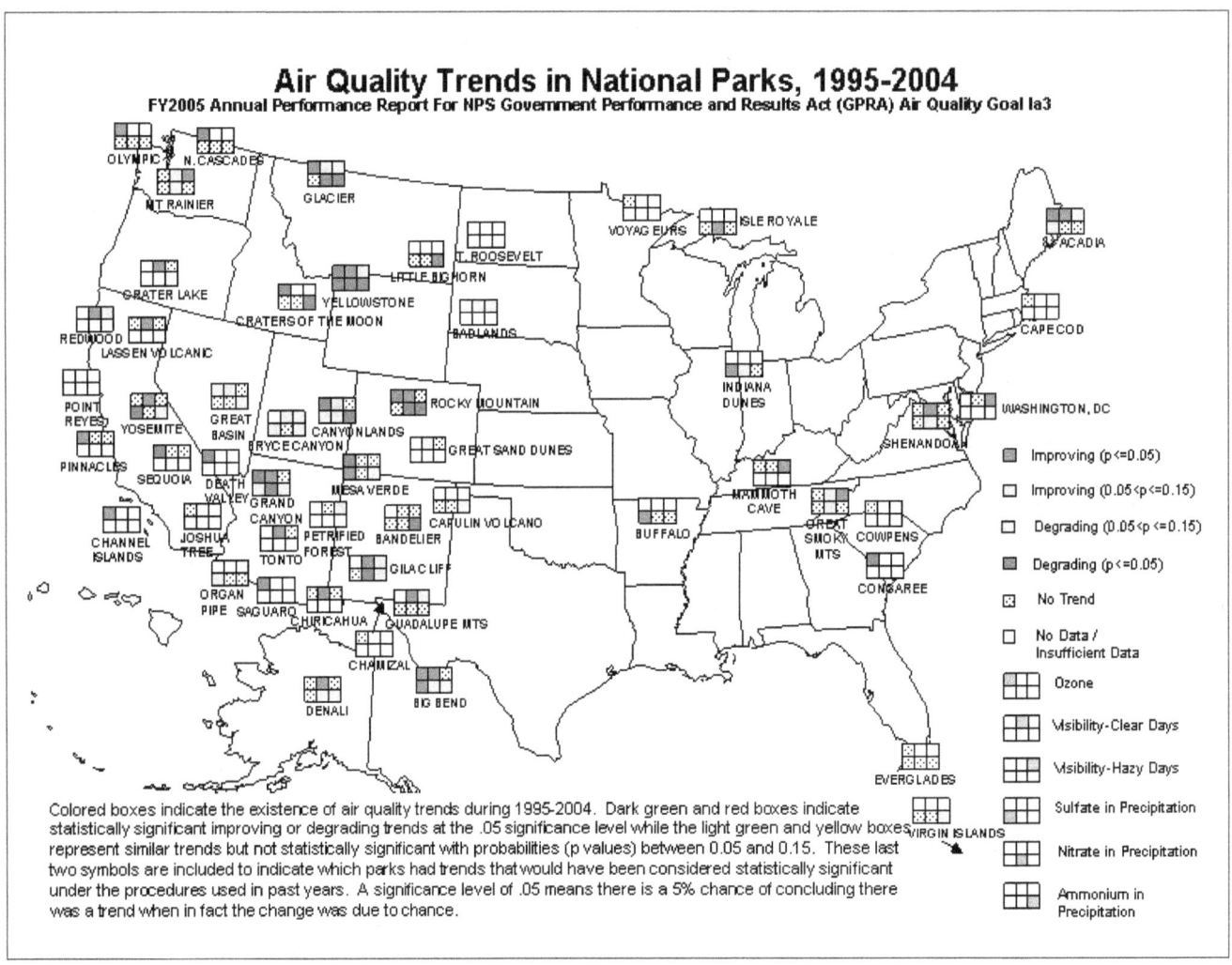

Figure G1. Air quality trends in national parks, 1995–2004 (NPS 2006a).

Atmospheric deposition

The following discussion uses both NADP and CAST-Net data to describe atmospheric deposition at Chirica-hua National Monument.

Regional patterns

Spatial patterns of sulfur (from sulfate) and nitrogen (from nitrate and ammonium) from precipitation in 2004 appear in Figures G2 (concentrations) and G3 (deposition). Sulfate concentrations and depositions were generally lower in the West (including the SODN) than in the East, reflecting regional differences in sulfur dioxide emissions (primarily from coal-burning power plants). Nitrate concentrations had notable "hotspots"

in the Midwest and Intermountain West, including CHIR and other portions of the SODN. Nitrate forms from emissions of nitrogen oxides from vehicles, power plants, and other combustion sources. Ammonium concentrations from agricultural activities were high throughout the central plains, reaching to the Colorado Front Range. Total nitrogen deposition (nitrate and ammonium) was highest throughout the Midwest, as a result of a combination of higher ammonium and nitrate concentrations and higher rainfall. As noted above, the GPRA report indicated that nitrogen deposition was increasing in several areas of the Intermountain West. During 1985–2002, nitrate concentrations in rainfall increased from 25–50% in the SODN region; ammonium increased more than 50% (Lehmann et al. 2005).

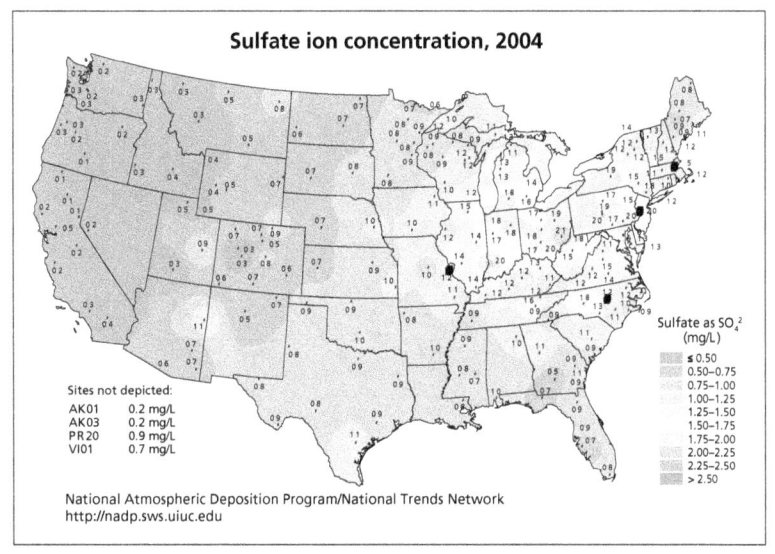

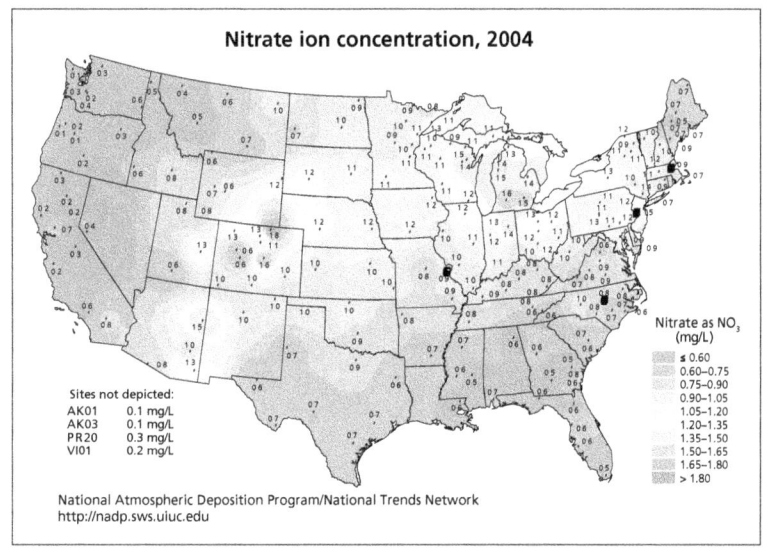

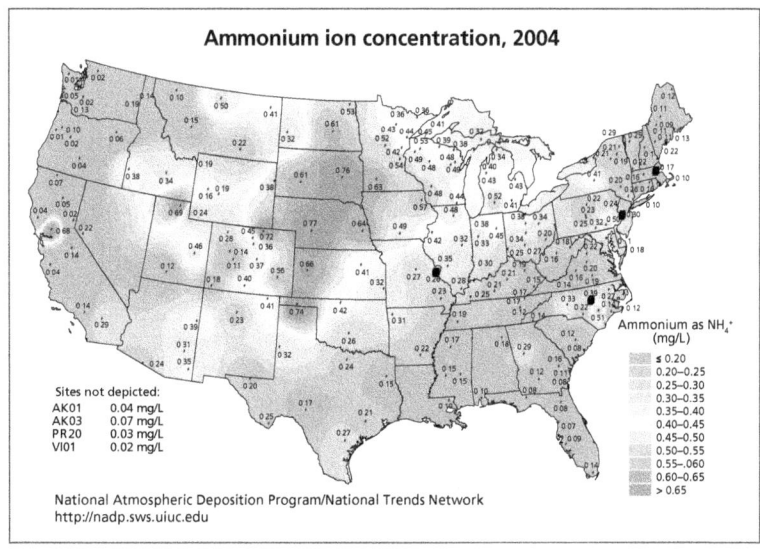

Figure G2. Spatial distribution of sulfate, nitrate, and ammonium concentrations for 2004 (NADP 2005).

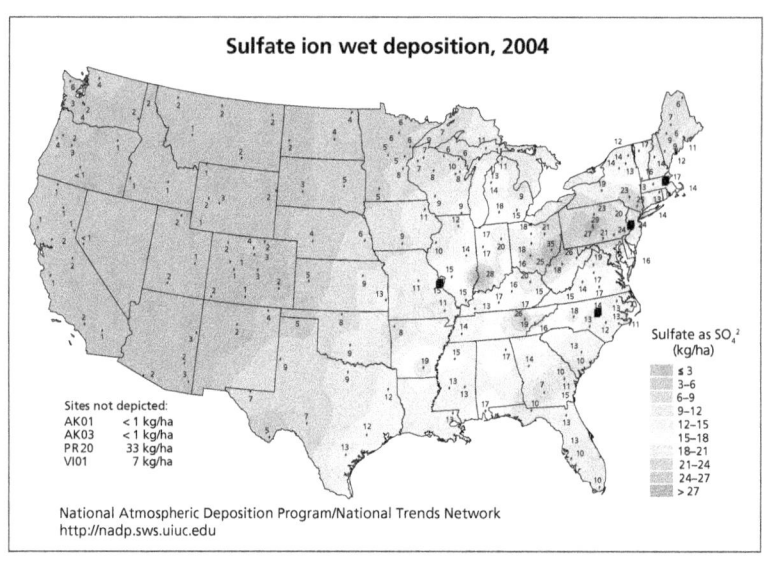

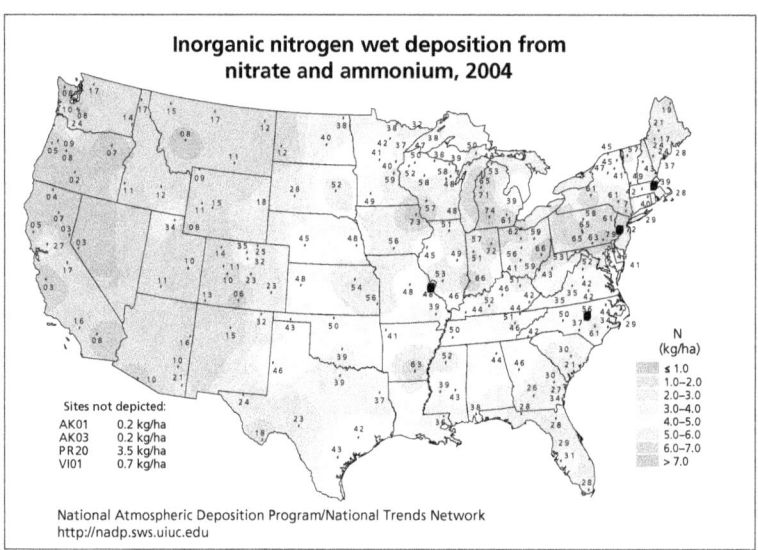

Figure G3. Spatial distribution of sulfate and nitrogen deposition for 2004 (NADP 2005).

Site trends

Concentrations in rainfall are used to examine temporal trends, as concentrations are generally independent of rainfall amount. At CHIR, concentrations of sulfate appeared stable in the period 2000–2004; nitrate and ammonium appeared to be increasing (Figure G4).

CASTNet also reports trends in deposition. As noted above, variations in rainfall from year to year make it difficult to discern short-term (5-year) trends. Long-term trends (>10 years) may be easier to distinguish. Figure G5 summarizes trends in wet and dry (total) nitrogen and sulfur deposition for the period 1992–2004 in CHIR.

Because the NADP site did not start operating until 1999, CASTNet used regional estimates for 1992–1999. Total sulfur deposition appeared to be decreasing; total nitrogen deposition appeared to be slightly increasing.

The pie charts in Figure G6 depict the composition of nitrogen and sulfur deposition at CHIR during 2002–2004. These estimates suggest that wet deposition exceeded dry deposition. However, the CASTNet method may underestimate dry deposition. Nitrate and ammonium contributed almost equally to total nitrogen deposition at the site.

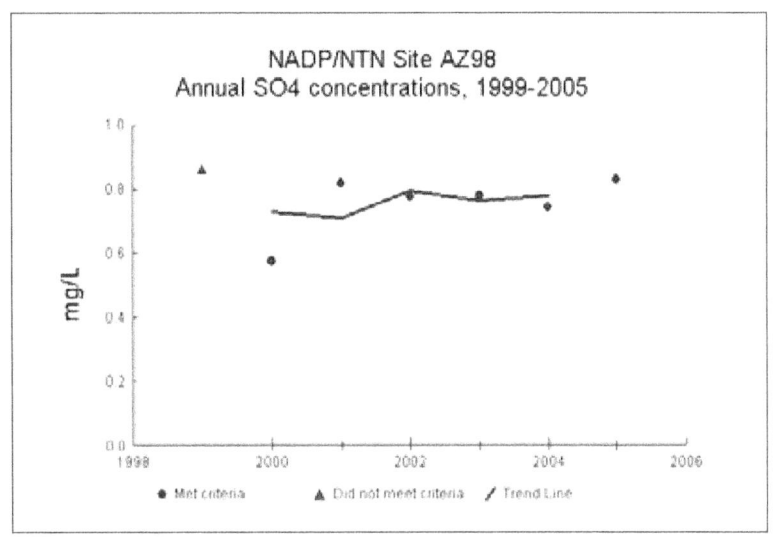

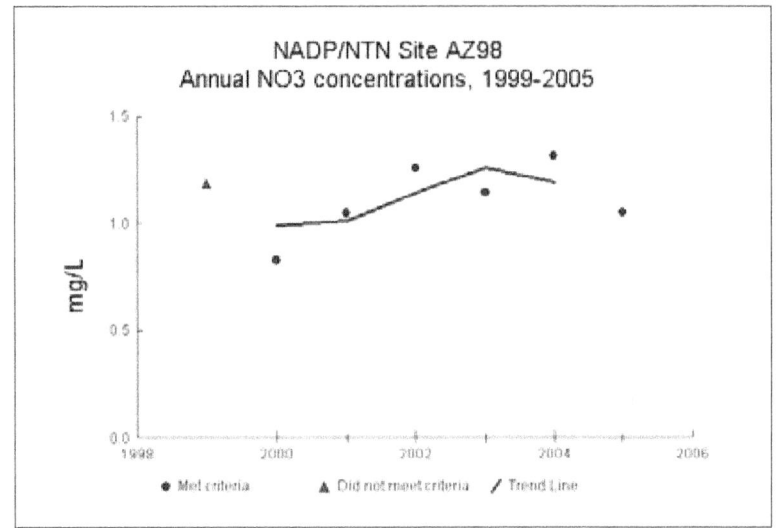

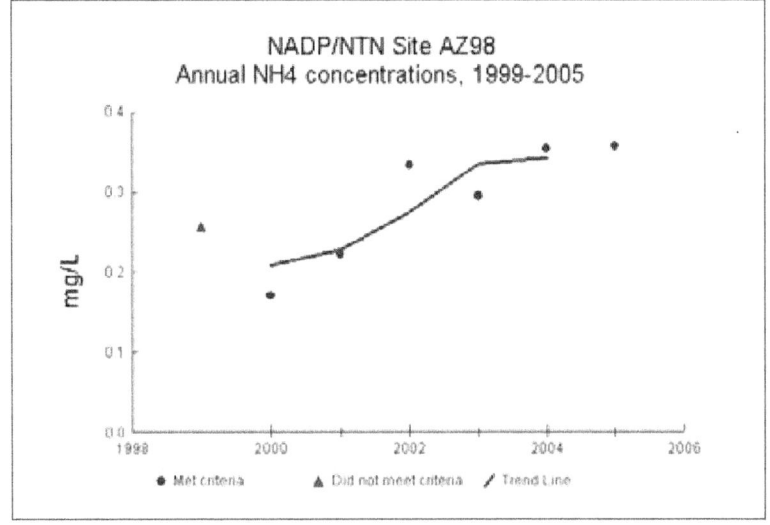

Figure G4. Trend lines (composed of a three-year, centered, weighted-moving average value) for concentrations of sulfate, nitrate, and ammonium in wet deposition at Chiricahua NM, 1999–2004 (NADP 2005).

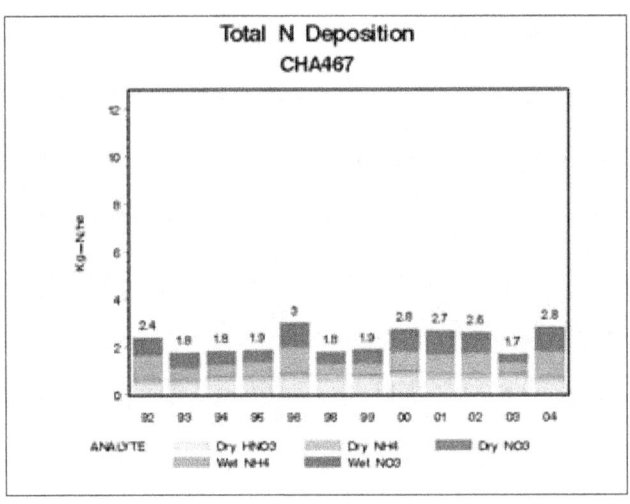

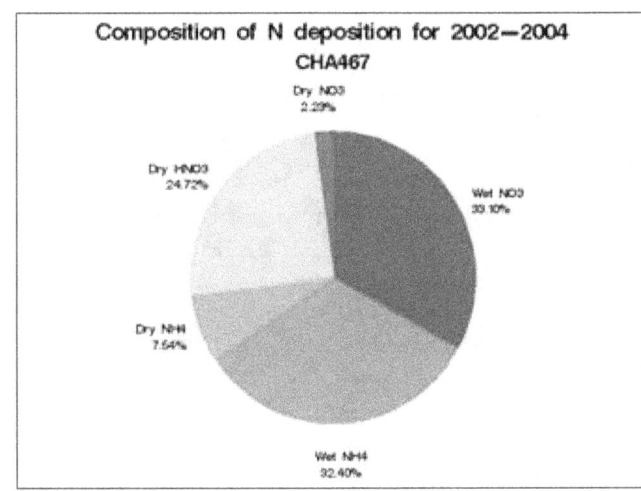

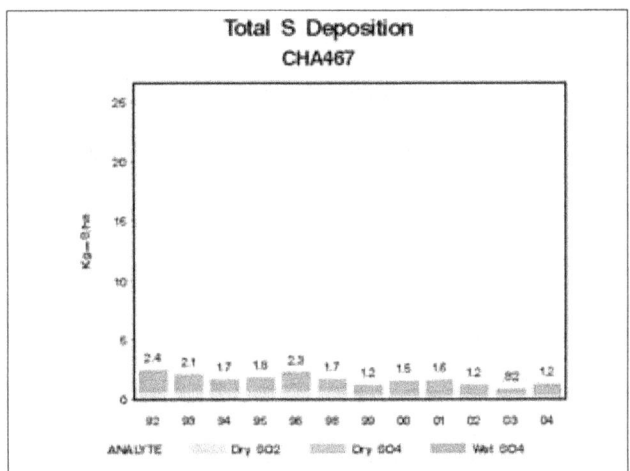

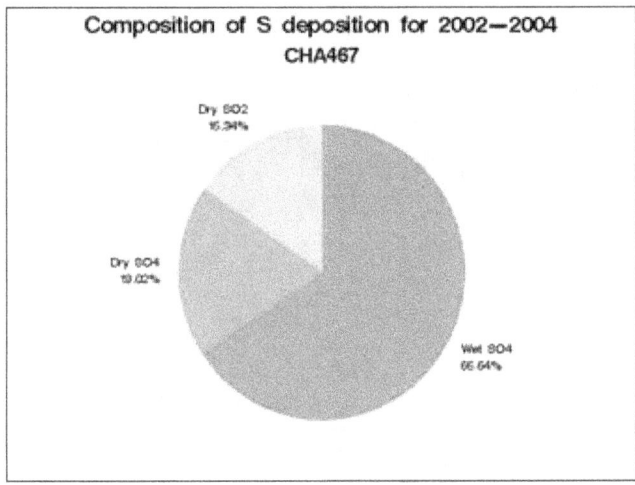

Figure G5. Trends in total nitrogen and sulfur deposition at Chiricahua NM, 1992–2004 (EPA 2005).

Figure G6. Contributions of wet and dry chemical species to total deposition at Chiricahua NM, 2002–2004 (EPA 2005).

Ozone

Ground-level ozone has been monitored in Chiricahua NM from 1992 to the present. In 2004, data capture was 99% for the monitor (NPS–ARD 2005). CHIR ozone summary data for 2004 is provided in Table G2.

No exceedances were recorded in CHIR from 1992 to the present (NPS 2006b). The fourth-highest 8-hour ozone concentration for 2004 was 70 ppb, below the standard of 85 ppb. CHIR demonstrated no trend in the three-year average fourth-highest 8-hour ozone concentration from 1994 to 2003 (NPS–ARD 2005).

The ozone risk assessment (NPS–ARD 2004) for CHIR concluded that vegetation in the park was considered at low risk from ozone injury.

Visibility

Spatial and seasonal trends

Chiricahua National Monument is characterized by good visibility (Figure G7). The average light extinction for the 20% clearest days in CHIR in 2004 was 5.8 Mm^{-1} (Table G3); the average light extinction for the 20% haziest days in 2004 was 21.2 Mm^{-1}. The State of Arizona is currently developing visibility improvement goals for its Class I areas, including CHIR, in consultation with the NPS.

Some seasonal patterns were evident in light extinction at Chiricahua NM in 2004 (Figure G8), with extinction being highest in the summer months and lowest in the winter months.

Site trends

Light extinction trends are shown in Figure G9. The GPRA analysis found that on the 20% clearest days, visibility significantly improved in CHIR from 1994–2003. On the 20% haziest days, visibility remained stable.

Composition

Figure G10 shows the contribution of various haze components for 2003, a year with particularly high light extinction on hazy days. On some of the days with very high extinction, soil (e.g., windblown dust) and/or organic matter (e.g., wildland fires) were the dominant factors. Sulfate remained a strong contributor at nearly all times.

Table G2. Ozone concentrations (parts per billion-ppb) and exposure indices summaries for Chiricahua NM in 2004.

Park code	Number of 8-hr concentrations at >85 ppb	First-highest 8-hr concentrations	Fourth-highest 8-hr* concentrations	Second-highest 1-hr concentrations	SUM06** (ppm-hr)	W126*** (ppm-hr)	N100 (#hr > 100 ppb)
CHIR	0	75	70	78	24.7	39.9	0

(NPS-ARD 2005)

* The National Ambient Air Quality Standard for ozone is 85 ppb, based on the three-year average of the fourth-highest daily maximum 8-hour average ozone concentration.

** The running 90-day maximum sum of the 0800–2000 hourly concentrations of ozone equal to or greater than 0.06 ppm.

Table G3. Annual average light extinction on the 20% clearest and 20% haziest days in 2004 at Chiricahua NM.

	Average value (Mm^{-1})
Clearest 20%	5.4
Haziest 20%	21.2

(from http://vista.cira.colostate.edu/views/web/AnnualSummaryDev/Trends.aspx. Accessed 3 Feb 2006)

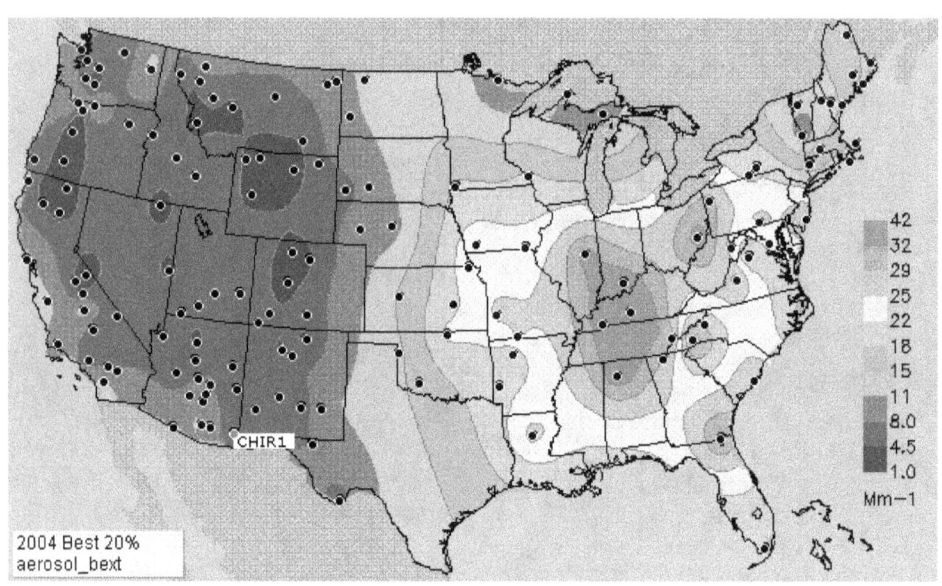

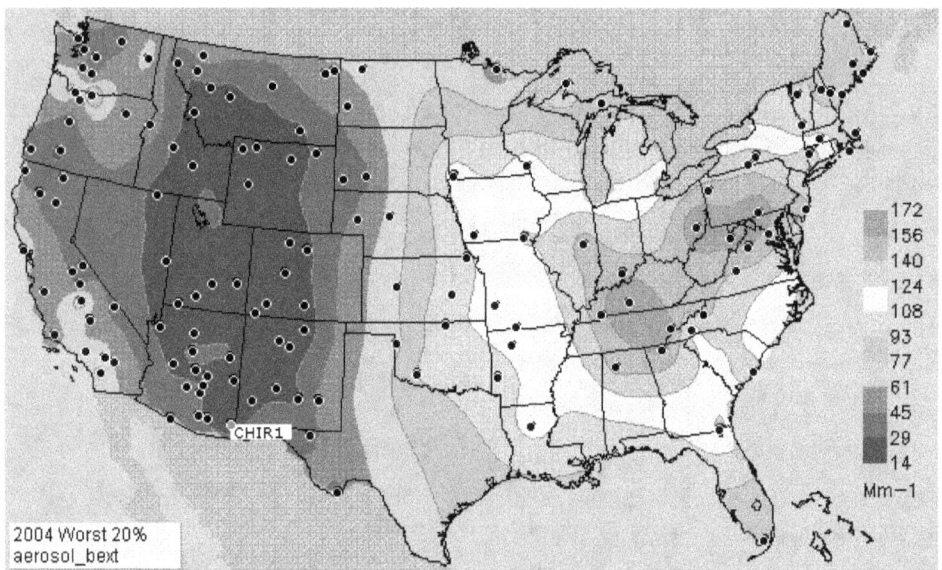

Figure G7. Spatial distribution of aerosol light extinction on the 20% clearest days (above) and the 20% haziest days (below) in 2004 (VIEWS 2006).

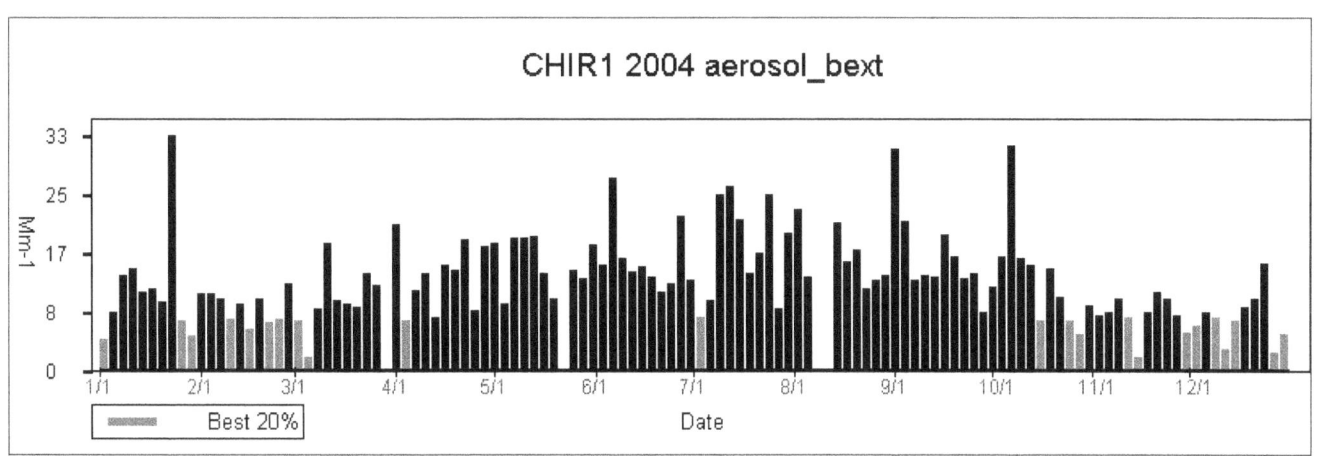

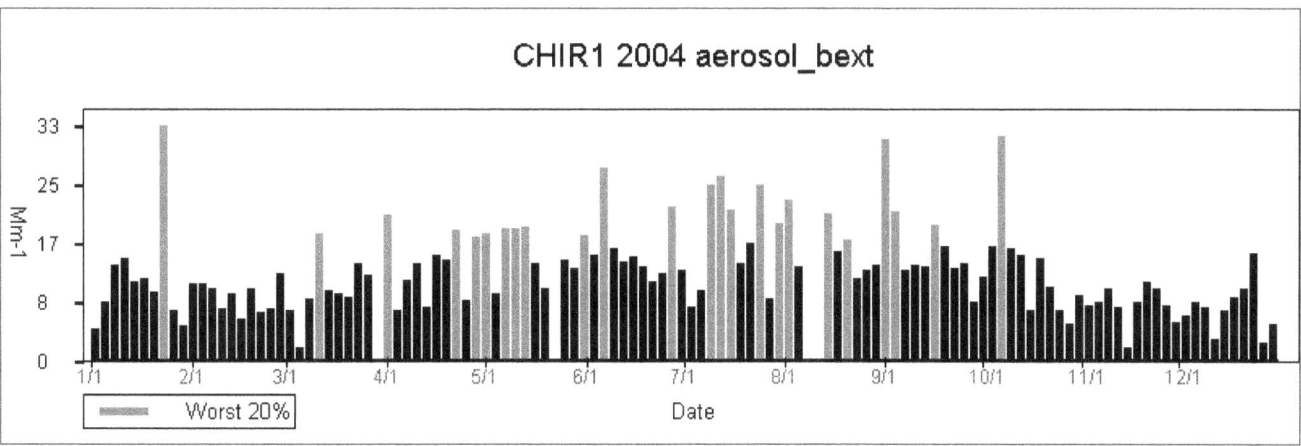

Figure G8. Seasonal patterns in aerosol light extinction on the 20% clearest (above) and haziest (below) days in 2004 at Chiricahua NM (VIEWS 2006).

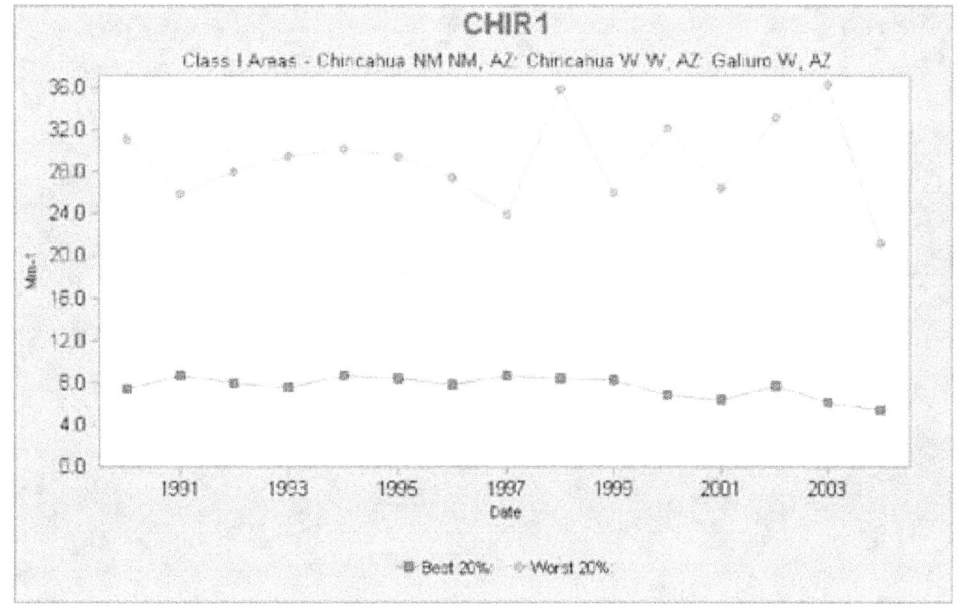

Figure G9. Trends in aerosol light extinction on the 20% clearest days and the 20% haziest days at Chiricahua NM (VIEWS 2006).

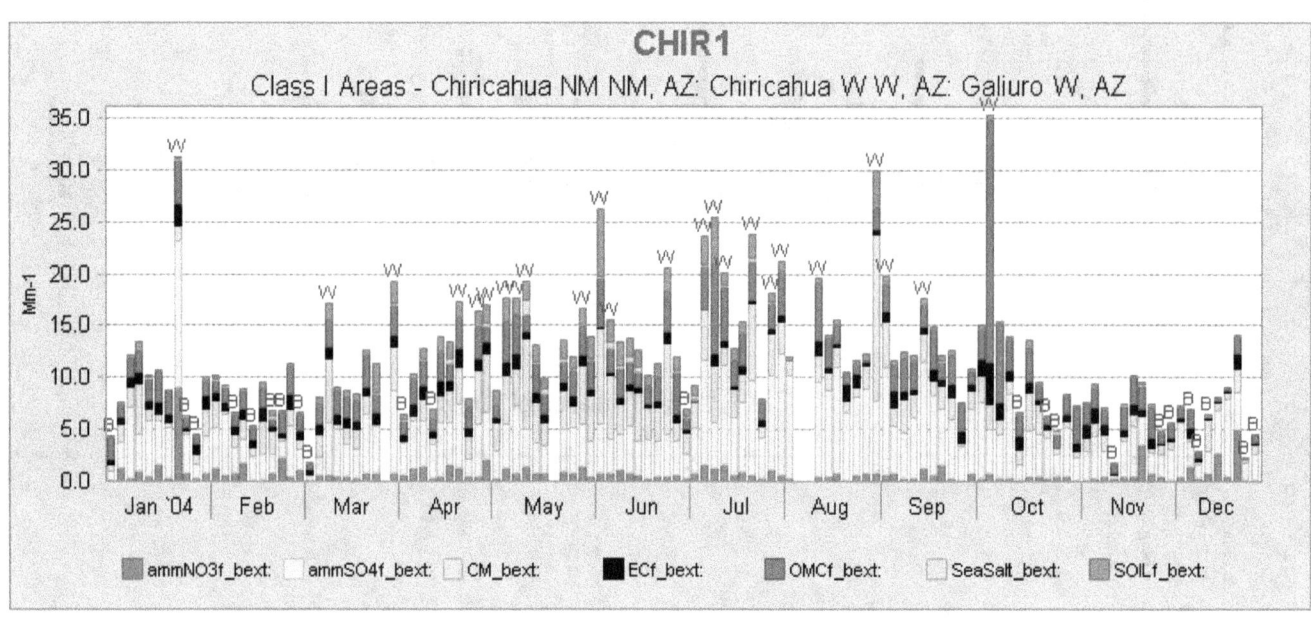

Figure G10. Seasonal patterns in haze composition at Chiricahua NM in 2004 (VIEWS 2006).

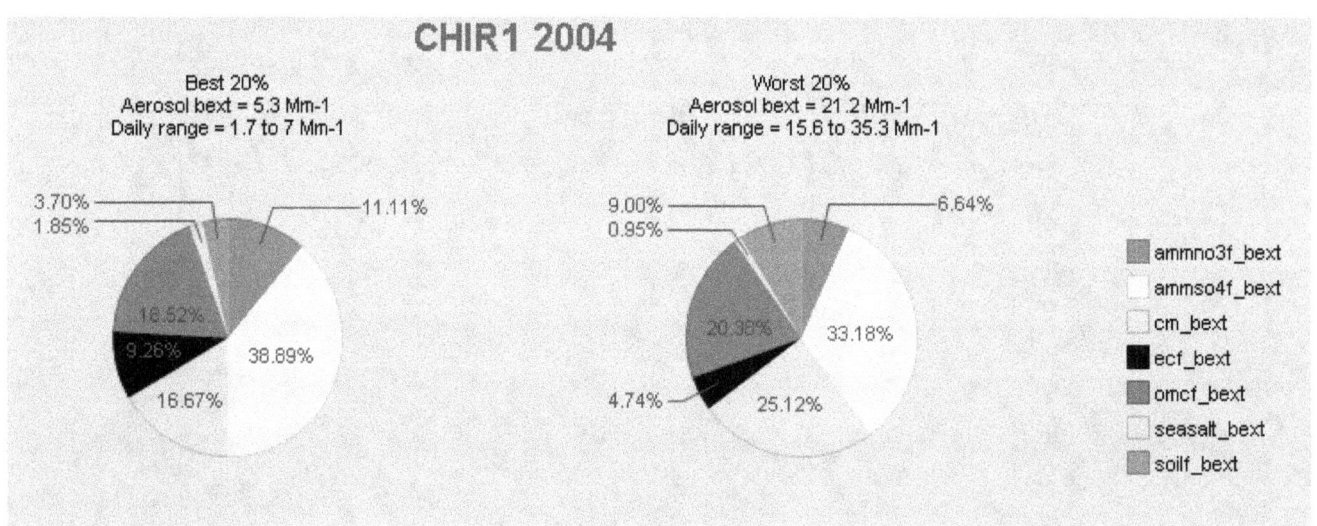

Figure G11. Pie charts showing composition of fine particles at Chiricahua NM in 2004 (VIEWS 2006).

Discussion and Conclusions

Atmospheric deposition

Long-term trends for atmospheric deposition are not yet available for CHIR. However, GPRA long-term trends for nearby sites indicate that sulfur deposition (measured by wet sulfate) in the Southwest is generally stable, while nitrogen deposition (measured by wet nitrate and ammonium) is increasing in several areas. Short-term trendlines from the NADP suggest that sulfate concentrations in precipitation in CHIR were stable from 2000–2004, while nitrate and ammonium concentration increased. Total sulfur deposition, as estimated by CASTNet using both CASTNet and NADP data, was approximately 1 kg/ha/yr; total nitrogen deposition was from 2.5–3.0 kg/ha/yr. Sulfur and nitrogen deposition were significantly elevated above natural background deposition, which is estimated to be 0.25 kg/ha/yr for either sulfur or nitrogen.

Ecosystems in CHIR are not likely to be affected by sulfur deposition, which primarily causes acidification of sensitive, poorly buffered waters and soils. However, ecosystems in CHIR may be sensitive to elevated nitrogen deposition.

Ozone

Ozone in Chiricahua NM appeared unchanged for the period 1995–2004. No exceedances of the EPA's ozone standard were recorded from 1992–2004. In 2004, the fourth-highest 8-hour average concentration was 70 ppb, approximately 82 of the EPA's standard of 85 ppb.

Risk to vegetation in CHIR is likely to be low, because ozone peak concentrations rarely reach high levels (i.e., above 100 ppb). In addition, dry conditions in CHIR are likely to limit ozone uptake. If ozone concentrations and exposures increase, the risk of ozone injury will increase, especially in years with adequate moisture.

Visibility

Visibility on the clearest days is improving in CHIR; visibility on the haziest days is stable. Clear days occur generally in the cooler months, hazy days in the warmer months. Windblown dust, organics, and sulfate are significant contributors to haze in CHIR.

References

Brooks, M. 2003. Effects of increased soil nitrogen on the dominance of alien annual plants in the Mojave Desert. Journal of Applied Ecology 40:344–353.

Environmental Protection Agency (EPA). 2005. http://www.epa.gov/castnet/).

Fenn, M., J. Baron, E. Allen, H. Rueth, K. Nydick, L. Geiser, W. Bowman, J. Sickman, T. Meixner, D. Johnson, and P. Neitlich. 2003. Ecological effects of nitrogen deposition in the western United States. BioScience 53:404–420.

Lehmann, C., V. Bowersox, and S. Larson. 2005. Spatial and temporal trends of precipitation chemistry in the United States, 1985–2002. Environmental Pollution 135:347–361.

National Atmospheric Deposition Program (NADP). 2005. 2004 annual summary. http://nadp.sws.uiuc.edu/lib/data/2004as.pdf. Last accessed February 14, 2007.

National Park Service (NPS). 2005. 2005 annual performance & progress report: Air quality in national parks. http://www2.nature.nps.gov/air/Pubs/pdf/gpra/Gpra2005_Report_03202006_Final.pdf. Last accessed February 14, 2007.

——. 2006a. Performance measures. http://www2.nature.nps.gov/air/who/npsPerfMeasures.cfm. Last accessed February 14, 2007.

——. 2006b. Ozone standard exceedances in national parks. http://www2.nature.nps.gov/air/Monitoring/exceed.cfm. Last accessed February 14, 2007.

——. 2006c. Natural resource year in review–2005. http://www2.nature.nps.gov/yearinreview/PDF/YIR2005_01.pdf. Last accessed February 14, 2007.

National Park Service–Air Resources Division (NPS–ARD). 2002. Air Quality in the National Parks, 2nd Edition. National Park Service Air Resources Division, U.S. Department of the Interior, Lakewood, CO.

——. 2004. Assessing the risk of foliar injury from ozone on vegetation in parks in the Sonoran Desert Network. October. http://www2.nature.nps.gov/air/Pubs/pdf/03Risk/sodnO3RiskOct04.pdf. Last accessed February 14, 2007.

——. 2005. FY2004 annual performance report: Government Performance and Results Act (GPRA). http://www2.nature.nps.gov/air/who/npsPerfMeasures.cfm. Last accessed February 14, 2007.

Visibility Information Exchange Web System (VIEWS). 2006. http://vista.cira.colostate.edu/views/Web/AnnualSummary/ContourMaps.aspx.

NPS D-60, April 2007

National Park Service
U.S. Department of the Interior

Natural Resource Program Center
1201 Oak Ridge Drive, Suite 150
Fort Collins, Colorado 80525

www.nature.nps.gov